In Time Like Glass

In Time
Like Glass

Reflections on a Journey in Asia

Evelyn Ames

with drawings by Joe Veno

HOUGHTON MIFFLIN COMPANY BOSTON

1974

The quotation on page 21 from "Burnt Norton" is reprinted by permission of Harcourt Brace Jovanovich from *Four Quartets* by T. S. Eliot.

First Printing v

Library of Congress Cataloging in Publication Data

Ames, Evelyn Perkins.
   In time like glass.

   1. Asia—Description and travel—1951–   2. Ames,
Evelyn Perkins. I. Title.
DS10.A396   915.4'04'50924 [B]   74-10736
ISBN 0-395-19419-9

Printed in the United States of America

To all my guides and companions
on the inward journey

In many lands I have wandered,
and wondered, and listened, and seen;
And many my friends and companions,
and teachers and lovers have been.

. . . .

And I said to my soul in secret:
"Oh, thou who from journeys art come!
It is meet we should bear some token
of love to the stayers at home;

. . . .

I was loath from all that pleasaunce
of the Sun and his words and ways,
to come to my country giftless,
and showing no fruit of my days:

But if my hands were empty
of honey and pearls and gold,
There were treasures far sweeter than honey
and marvelous things to be told,

Whiter than pearls and brighter
than the cups at a Sultan's feast,
And these I have brought for love-tokens,
from the Lords of Truth, in my East.

> Saadi, from the *Gulistan*,
> (translated by Sir Edwin Arnold)

CONTENTS

INTRODUCTION

IN THE AUTUMN of 1971, I went with my husband on our first real visit to the Orient. Ten years earlier, business had taken us briefly to Japan but now, with no connections or experience with where we were going, we decided to join a small personally organized group. We were four American couples who, though having mutual friends, were strangers to one another and came from four different cities; our "guides" were an English couple who had spent a large part of their lives farming in Kenya, had traveled extensively and were now doing so as a business. Congenial companions who shared much, we were all of us in late middle age, our young families on their own; we were at that place in life where if you are still curious about the world — and lucky — you travel. Each couple had done so and we had, as well, the common bond of having made African tenting safaris and other moderately adventurous trips. This one was not — outwardly; we didn't ride yaks or camp out on the desert or cross mountain torrents on swaying rope bridges; we were quite ordinary tourists making a routine tour.

Why, then, a book about it? For one thing, because no two people make exactly the same journey: even if we visit identical places, my East and yours are just enough different to complement and enhance one another. Even more, however, the intensity of growing interest in the East, and the rapidity of the meeting between East and West, while too obvious to need comment, have such importance right now for the world's future that any grain of understanding, any direct perception from that other side of the world seems worth transmitting. To most Westerners Asia is still the far side of the moon and will probably remain so — the shadow that illustrates the round, each side needing the other.

A flying-carpet view, as ours was, of many different peoples, practices, architectures, religions all existing at once in today's world — is a gift of the jet. The very speed of transportation, in many ways so deplorable, also makes for a kind of quick mosaic, a vivid condensation of impressions approaching simultaneity. Like so much else it is an experience beyond the reach of language and to touch it at all with words would be presumptuous and absurd if it weren't (as a surprising number of people of different ages are observing) that the nature of time itself seems to be mysteriously changing and with it, the nature of experience. I wish it were possible to convey that sense of compression in an account, but we are limited to experiencing and expressing in a sequential way and it "takes" time even to look at a succession of pictures. Yet it seems to me that the writer, focusing on memories and uncluttered by the noise and distractions of travel itself, has some of the advantages of the skin diver exploring a reef. The diver puts on a mask and breathing tube, changes the angle of his vision by a few degrees and is over a different world. I, with that unfamiliar world of the East in the mind's eye, may be able to re-view and report on a journey now freed from time.

All journeys are adventures in time: to start out is to leave behind the usual time-sense as surely as it is to leave well-known places, but this trip — on which we felt as if we penetrated the past more deeply than on any other yet taken — was also something more. Progressively, from Iran to Afghanistan, to Kashmir and Nepal and India, we seemed to move into some other dimension altogether, not only of history and back through the ages, which happens in other parts of the world, but like entering a new kind of space. I even heard myself saying, a few days after our return, that coming back was like returning from outer space — no, I quickly corrected myself: from inner space. Hearing the words (which had spoken themselves), I wondered why I had used them, what I meant by them. Evidently this journey had been not only geographical and cultural; wherever else we had been was indeed "strange as Asia" and stranger than I'd expected.

I went somewhat prepared, having read fairly widely and for many years in the field of Eastern religions and thought, and being fortunate in having as friends such leaders as Alan Watts, Nancy Wilson Ross and the remarkable Ruth Sasaki — American widow of a Zen sage and, herself, the abbess of a temple outside Kyoto. I had tried Zen meditation and decided I wasn't up to its particular rigors but the Zen "way," as I found it, made life more alive and caused no conflicts with what I believed; it was as natural, fresh and vivid as its typical haiku; it was intensely human.

On a quite different — one might say visceral — level, Indian myths and symbols fascinated me and I longed to visit the country of their source. Without being exactly a pilgrim, which would in any case have been impossible under the circumstances, I was very much open to the East and full of anticipation.

This anticipation, or possibly something less explicable, brought about a series of personal events which I relate because of their connection to the meaning the trip had for me. They began two weeks before departure with a dream in which one of those priestly and oracular figures that haunt the dream world presented me with a dish garden, or terrarium, planted with moss and ground pine and bright woods berries. In the middle of this stood a glass bell, or dome, and under it, perfect in every detail, grew two of what I recognized as fly agaric, or *Amanita muscaria*, mushrooms — the typical glowingly red or orange toadstools of fairy tales — encrusted with frosty white warts and knobs. Without understanding why, I felt sure, as one does with certain dreams, that it was of singular importance and that this offering was somehow connected with the journey we were about to make.

In the few days we spent in Switzerland on our way to the East, the dream kept resonating, in such reminders as coming upon people out mushrooming in the woods; finding the daughter of friends photographing mushrooms indoors, in an arranged setting of moss and leaves; and — the afternoon before we flew to Iran — a strange happening. Out of a collection of last-minute purchases, my husband unwrapped and showed to me a bright new paperback he had bought, on the cover of which were the two red mushrooms, one big, one small, that I knew so well. It wasn't the first time I have dreamed something vivid and a touch bizarre (which is typical of so-called precognitive dreams) and then proceeded to see it in real life, nor did this garish picture have any of the

overtones of my dream mushrooms; still, like the sound of a
fingernail flicked against a glass, it set up a faint, clear ringing.

What on earth did mushrooms have to do with where we
were going? More than I knew until long after our return,
when a random, zigzag trail of things read and heard led me
to read remarkable new findings about the fly agaric. One of
the hallucinatory mushrooms, it is now thought to be the basis
of the mysterious and divine "Soma" celebrated in hymn after
hymn of the *Rig-Veda* — that most ancient collection of
Hindu sacred verses. And this plant substance which the
Vedic priests used in their rituals (and even worshiped as a
divinity because of its miraculous powers) was collected in
the mountains of Iran, the Hindu Kush, the Himalayas.

All mushrooms, of whatever form or color, have a kind of
primitive magic, springing unpredictably as they do out of
hidden spawn, smelling of the earth, and some with the
capacity to induce visions. It seems probable to me now that
my dream mushrooms represented mysteries that would be
shown to me on the journey yet remain inaccessible: they
were covered by the glass of cultural differences; under some
conditions they could be harmful. What I saw can also be
interpreted as a highly graphic illustration of "inner space":
the mushroom mysteries growing in a space separated and
protected from the rest of the world by the "glass" division
between conscious and unconscious mind, between inner and
outer reality.

Both interpretations fit the rather special meaning the trip
came to hold: the strong sense of connectedness to what was
extremely alien, which sprang up spontaneously and could
never be quite accounted for; the unexpected intimations
coming out of the depths of the unknown, which could not

be actually grasped. For on several occasions in our travels, the most solidly real people and places, temples and mountains seemed like manifestations of another, invisible reality, as if they were descriptions or extensions of it; the visible, tangible world suddenly become a metaphor. These were not visions, or hallucinations, and they are hard to describe yet they are part of one person's experience and a basis for speculations which have general concern. They — and a wish rather like that of the poet Saadi's: to bring "some token . . . to the stayers at home" — are what made me want to tell the story.

Threshold of the East

GATE OF ALL NATIONS

I WAS WAKENED by a voice. A man's voice, outdoors somewhere, not exactly singing but intoning the same loud unintelligible phrase over and over. Struggling up out of layers of sleep and postflight exhaustion, I slowly realized it must be a street vendor calling his wares. The room, when I opened my eyes, was blazing bright, the air coming in through gently moving curtains stunningly hot. I got up and looked out. Six stories down in a narrow, cobbled alley between buildings, a man walked slowly along beside a white donkey carrying two baskets mounded with melons. Women were coming out of doorways and while I watched a sale was made. Then another voice came down the alley, the calls getting gradually louder and nearer; this time an old man with an open basket on his arm in which lay a few eggs as if in a nest. Selling food from door to door, on foot? In a city of three and a half million which, as you fly over it at night, looks almost like Los Angeles?

The buildings across the alley were three or four stories high; I could see over miles of city — sand-colored or white, blocky, flat as the flattest beach. The light was blinding and hazy, both, the way it is when sand is blowing, so that at first I couldn't make out and then couldn't believe the faint outline of mountains halfway up the sky, apparently rising straight out of Tehran itself. A wave of heat brought the smell of the air, totally different from any smell I knew, different even from that of Damascus the night before, where we hadn't been allowed to deplane but had stood in the open door as if at the entrance to a greenhouse. The air here was drier, spicier, astringent; perhaps it was the special smell of the Orient I'd heard about since childhood from my much traveled father, or my uncle who lived forty years in China. Something else Father had mentioned about the East — "the sense of confusion and excitement in crowds of people naturally more expressive and noisy than people in the West" — we had already discovered, having arrived at the airport at the same time as three jumbo jetloads of Assyrians being repatriated, each passenger being met by ten or twenty relatives and friends. The newspapers estimated that several thousand were in the air terminal and we could have added that everything else was excessive: the vehemence, confusion and violent shoving as well as the unexpected kindness, even tenderness, from strangers that suddenly let in a little hope that one would, eventually, reach the inner room and customs counter, the outdoors beyond.

The wide streets and boulevards of Tehran that night were a strange spectacle, in the process of being decorated for the celebrations, two weeks away, of the 2500th Anniversary of the Persian Empire. Fantastic constructions like those at World Fairs loomed up unlit in the middle of traffic circles and even at one in the morning laborers were at work on them. Along the entire way from the airport to our hotel, each street and thoroughfare was arched over every hundred yards by frameworks for lighting. Though these were still dark, we could make out as we drove under them miles of fountains, of peacocks with spread tails, portraits of the Shah and Empress circled with flowers.

Being in Iran for the first time during this precelebration period gave us unusual impressions, for in each city we visited, each village we drove through, everyone's attention was on cleaning up, painting, putting up decorations — some exquisite, others gaudy. It was like preparing for Christmas but on an astronomical scale since it was to cost over three hundred million dollars. The purpose of the celebration, people kept saying, was to "raise the nation's pride in its glorious heritage," which is the kind of rhetoric such occasions demand though before we left the country it came to mean more.

Iran, when you look at the map, is a bridge between Central Asia and India to the east, the Levant and Europe to the west. It has been repeatedly swept by migrations, invaders and conquerors from both directions; it has had its religion, its script and even its language (partly) changed yet somehow always retained a strong identity of its own. At the end of no more than one week there we felt we knew why: the Iranians we saw seemed the most confident, independent and easy people in the world. At their best it made them warm and outgoing, at their worst, disagreeably stubborn; evidently they have always resisted whatever they didn't care to adopt, and adapted out of strength rather than weakness to what they did want.

While we were there, the Empress Farah stated as one of her chief wishes for Iran, "to safeguard its culture and civilization from the negative effects of the industrialized West." Many of her country's prevailing conditions, including its environment, climate and other factors, she said, "are not conducive to an all-out adoption of Western civilization."

Her words were heavy with meaning for us. Only a few days earlier, our host in Switzerland — a thoughtful, widely traveled and scientifically trained man — had said in a shockingly matter-of-fact voice: "I think we are seeing the *latter* stages of the rapid decline of Western civilization"; and he repeated "rapid decline" for emphasis. We were enjoying a picnic at the time in one of the high *alpages* where cattle are pastured in the summer months; the cold mountain air was musical with the clanging harmonies of cowbells, the underlying sound all around us of small, invisible streams. If you lived here, in this valley, he had speculated, you might be able to survive, grow most of what you needed and live off the land, though it would be hard. "People will survive here and there, I think, in little pockets like this one."

None of us said anything to that; the statement hung there, to be echoed in a phrase of the herdsman we spoke with later who thought he would be taking his cattle down the mountain any day now. Squinting up at the impossible cliffs, the flying clouds overhead, he added: *"On sent l'automne qui vient . . ."*

How much more melancholy, more ominous it sounds in French than in English! The end of far more than a season hovered over us there, as it did now on reading the young Empress's views, and would again with any confrontation between the ancient world we were moving into and the industrialized West we were leaving behind.

Hardly more than twenty-four hours after arriving, we began learning about Iran's environment, on one of the dawn flights common in that part of the world. Over last-minute

packing and a last gulp of coffee, dead tired still, I protested
bitterly this getting up before the sun, though it is the sun's
heat and the resulting turbulence over desert country that
makes these early flights necessary. All the way to Shiraz we
flew over desert — lion-colored, bare, humping up into
mountains of rock: "the most terrible country I've ever seen,"
said one of our companions, shaking her head. There were
occasional faint signs of green around settlements but even the
mud villages with their little square houses looked like something children shape out of wet sand and leave to dry. How
did people *live?* Only because of the *qanats* — those bril-
liantly engineered water courses which lead water underground from the surrounding mountains to villages and fields,
underground so that none will be sucked away by the furiously dry air. The whole scheme, which was invented over
two thousand years ago and remains utterly practical, works
by gravity; getting exactly the right tilt for the channel,
building and maintaining it is an intricate, highly respected
skill. All that shows from above is a line of craters at
regular intervals, marking the entrances into the tunnel — no
bigger when seen from a plane than the air holes in beach sand
made by tiny marine creatures.

In the middle of this desert, in a setting of bony hills, lies
the oasis city of Shiraz, punctuated with cypresses and palms,
the air sweet from the millions of roses growing along its wide
boulevards and in countless gardens. An easy, gentle-feeling
place over which the sky-colored domes of four mosques float
like bubbles on the surface of a pebbly pool. When they visit
here, the Shah and his Empress stay in a little fantasy of a
palace, which looks quite unreal and as if constructed of
starched embroidery and lace, placed in a beautifully kept

garden. One visit to a Persian garden (and this capital of the province of Fars, the ancient "Parsa," cradle of the Empire, *is* Persia) and Persian prints and design and poetry come suddenly alive. In blazing dry country, water, color and shade satisfy several of the senses at once and not just one; the body that has shut itself against heat and glare and dust feels relaxed and expansive. Also, in the Eram gardens, as in each one we visited, the strict symmetry of water channels, like the lines of cypresses and formal flower beds, are a delicious relief from the apparently limitless and formless distances beyond. We did find one informal corner, where we sat and rested in the shade of a hugely spreading tree rather like a maple which our guide, Hamadi, told us was the heart of every Persian garden. "The loved place," he called it.

Hamadi had thick black eyebrows, a bushy mustache and very white teeth; he looked more like a well-born and prosperous merchant than a guide and was well enough off to have acquired a fine collection of carpets and built himself an attractive house, to which he invited our whole party of ten for "tea." We sat in a circle on the living-room floor and were served by him and his young wife: tea with sugar cookies and sweet fruit paste, followed by corn on the cob (it tasted just like ours), which had been roasted over charcoal and dipped into salted hot water. From out in the hall, where several of Hamadi's men friends helped prepare this, voluble talk and laughter accompanied the sizzling and hissing of steam. The last course was chunks of melon, the flesh paler than honeydew and streaming with juice, then Hamadi brought in a hookah and the pipe was passed, bubbling cozily, around the circle. He was not only a good host, he seemed completely at ease with us, having the confidence and dignity which made it unnecessary either to try to impress us or to be in the least servile.

In the Bazaar of Shiraz we were among hundreds of his countrymen. Almost the only foreigners there that morning, Amyas and I caused consternation, turning sometimes to adoration of our appearance, particularly our blue eyes. We are both of us tall and Nordic-looking, my hair white and fluffy; to them we couldn't look more different. In the little open-fronted shops raised above the pavement, groups of men sat around their hubble-bubbles like figures on a stage, staring at us as much as we did at them, particularly at me since I was not only foreign but a woman without a veil. Near the entrance two young women in *chadors* — and almost every woman we saw wore this head-to-floor covering, which she held across the lower half of her face — stopped and gazed at me for several minutes with such love in their eyes it was like a love affair. It happened several times; beginning with amazement, relaxing when I smiled or made friendly eye-talk into warm response, growing into incandescent radiance, almost worship. Others were aloof — especially the nomadic Qashgai tribeswomen in their incredible clothes made of up to fifty yards of transparent gauzy stuff in brilliant colors striped and patterned with glitter. Almost every one of them carried in one arm what looked like a doll, dressed exactly like herself with the addition of a bonnet of gold or silver lace — only it was a baby, with huge expressive eyes, as all the children here have. Looking at these people, one has the sensation of going *into* their eyes, seeing far deeper into that person's being than is possible with the more closed and flat

iris of northern races. What do our eyes say to them? Are
they like some curious light-colored stone, an unfamiliar
agate?

The crush of strangers and expressions of curiosity in
foreign bazaars arouse a sense of claustrophobia in some
travelers — as they would in me at once if I felt any hostility — but where there are no political or historical grounds
for ill will, surely the more that different nationalities and
races are exposed to one another, the better. Left to themselves, without imposed prejudices, it is as natural for
strangers as for children to study one another, to try to
communicate in whatever way they can, and the greater the
polarity between them, the more intense the pleasure when a
connection is made — like the coupling of a fine image or
metaphor, where the farther apart are the things likened and
it still makes sense, the more deeply satisfying it is. Yet if this
is true for people in casual encounter or engaged in the same
activity, how instantly the magnetism may be reversed as soon
as anything depends on the connection: a thing or service to
be bought or sold, an agreement carried out, a hope fulfilled.
Expectation, in any form, between strangers as well as inti-
mates, is what rocks, or breaks the bridge.

What accounts for the gentle ease of Shiraz? Its location?
Something about its air or light? I knew a man who believed
people were the product of a place just like anything else it
grows — its particular fruit or cheese or wine. How else, he
speculated, can you account for a concentration of extraordinary musicians in the whole region around Odessa and not
just that city — a vintage crop of geniuses such as it turned
out around the turn of the century?

The culture of Fars culminated in two great poets — Hafiz,

the romantic, and Saadi, a mystic and aphorist. Both lie buried in exquisite shrines set in gardens, Saadi beside a deep spring that bubbles up underground at the foot of mountains covered with overlapping ledges of smooth rock like layers of armor. The wide, paved entrance to the shrine, like the steps and raised edge of the portico, is banked with hundreds of pots of carefully tended flowers; the colonnade in which the bier stands between arched openings, feels like a garden pavilion: birds fly through it. Lines from Saadi's poems, in the beautiful Iranian script, climb the vivid tiled walls like the stems and intricately twining tendrils of a vine. Hamadi recited them to us in Persian, followed with rough translations. While we listened, several women in faded *chadors* and with dirty feet approached the coffin reverently, rested their fingers on it and held their small children's hands against it. Touching a gravestone is traditional in Iran, but this reverence for a poet? And in poor and subjugated women? He must be a hero to them for his great humanity, his belief in the unity of man:

> *Limbs of a body are we, sons of men,*
> *Made from same clay, born of same origin.*
> *When one limb suffers by misfortune's stress*
> *Their fellows will not fare in happiness:*
> *Thou, who unmoved canst others' sorrows scan*
> *May be a monarch, but nowise a man.*

Saadi knew a lot about mankind. He really had three lives and in the second one, between the ages of forty and seventy, he wandered the earth. Through Afghanistan first, and down into India where he visited the temple of Shiva outside Bombay, then Delhi where he learned Hindustani. In the other direction he went as far as Abyssinia; he lived in Damascus for years and as a desert hermit outside Jerusalem; was taken prisoner there by invaders and put to hard labor in Tripoli; escaped and traveled from one end of North Africa to the other and across all of Asia Minor. Finally, at seventy, he returned to Shiraz to his third life, of poetry and contemplation, dying when he was over a hundred years old.

Men see the earth they travel over from two radically different points of view — that of observing and that of exploiting. The observers contemplate the endless richness and variety and strangeness of life — sometimes, as with Saadi or Herodotus or Marco Polo, to the world's lasting benefit. The others, driven by demonic forces as multi-limbed and -headed as those of deities in Hindu mythologies, have to possess and drain the earth, while the conquerors, like Genghis Khan and Tamerlane, consume and sweep away everything in their path, crossing continents like prairie fires. A few generations later, the scorched earth greens over again under the touch of some other remarkable being, whose urge is to create: Kubla Khan was Genghis' grandson.

I oversimplify. The contemplative artist and the total destroyer face in diametrically opposite directions and there are many in between, including conquerors such as Cyrus and Darius of Persia who, inspired with great ideas, create more than they exploit. On the Gate of All Nations at Persepolis, Darius had inscribed: "It is not my will that the strong should oppress the weak . . . God's plan for the earth is not turmoil but peace, prosperity, and good government."

Alexander burned Persepolis to ruins but the sculptured bas-reliefs depicting the realization of Darius' dreams — examples in stone of racial, religious and individual freedom — survive. Drifted over through the millennia with sand, they remain almost intact, like shells that miraculously survive storm tides. Going to Persepolis is to go to the heart of Persia — and to the heart of an idea which a large part of the world has been struggling toward ever since.

The day we went there, the road was lined for mile after mile and on both sides with lighted flares fed from barrels of kerosene. It seemed terribly wasteful, all those tongues of flame brightly flickering in the early morning sun, but this was the country of oil, I told myself, and maybe today the flares were just being tried out. In villages, decorations were being built and flags hung and wherever there were dumps or anything unsightly, walls were going up and being painted to hide them. On the bare hills nomads and shepherds moved with their flocks but everyone else in the countryside was focusing on the arrival of the Shah and the fifty heads of state coming to honor the Empire — a contemporary version of what it must have been when those first emperors and their courts — Darius and Xerxes and Ataxerxes — came here from the winter capital at Susa to celebrate the festival of Spring.

For the last fifteen miles the road runs perfectly straight across the level plain and apparently right into a bare, jagged mountain ahead. It is hard to see where there is room for a complex of palaces. Only when you are very near do the immensely tall and slender pillars begin to detach themselves from the background of the mountain, looking like a grove of bare tree trunks or a collection of chimneys left standing after buildings have been gutted by fire. The heart sinks with disappointment: what is impressive, or beautiful, about *this?*

Once you are up on the vast platform built out from the mountainside (and partly of it), it is clear why Darius set his

ritual city here. The panorama — a full hundred and eighty
degrees of it — with far waves of strange-shaped, ancient-
looking mountains, extends into unseen distances; the mountain at your back, like a rough-hewn building, supports the
terrace as if it were a giant viewing balcony. Not a tiptoe
place such as the Acropolis, nor a sky platform like Monte
Alban, but generous and open as arms spread out in welcome.
Overhead, in a sky intense as the deepest-toned Iranian turquoise, huge heads of bulls, eagles, horses, griffins — each
with its twin facing in the opposite direction — ride the tops
of sixty-foot columns, the "saddles" between the two heads
emptied of the beams they once carried, beams which were
cut out of whole cedars of Lebanon and placed to stretch
across an area of audience chambers as big as a football field.
The sense of majesty and magnificence begins, and a sense of
strangeness, too, before symbols vivid and unreal as dreams:
winged lion with faces of bearded men, eagles that have ears,
composite mythological beasts.

Mostly these are high up, or against sky — exactly where
they belong: crystallizations of thousands of nights of watching the stars in Leo and Taurus and Aquila, watching and
imagining and fearing. At one's feet, rows of pediments, faint
outlines of walls indicate space and size but no more. The
guide points them out and it is like being shown constellations
and trying to draw the right connecting lines in the mind:
here, the hall of a hundred columns; there, the entrance to the
inner audience chamber. So far it is mostly vast emptiness,
spaces presided over by those mysterious beasts, nothing to
human scale. Then one comes to the Apadana stairs.

Architects must always have known the powerful effect of
stairs, and in important public buildings they have used them

like commands. Those flights and flights up to senate chambers and courthouses that diminish a man, step by step, and force him to look up to authority! The steps up to the Parthenon — they are almost too big to be called that — and the ones on Mexican temples which are so steep, so narrow, climbing them is like clinging to the side of a mountain and you don't want to look down! The stairs at Persepolis are saying something about including people, not overpowering them: "It is not my will that the strong should oppress the weak." Even the steps of the Grand Staircase — the kind that divides partway up, turns in opposite directions and comes back to itself again — are easy, and the grade so gradual it is like walking up a gentle slope instead of the hundred and sixty feet it actually is: one is invited up to the platform above and in through the Gate of All Nations.

Through an outer hall and across a court, another gently graded double stairway leads to the Apadana or main audience chamber, the entire surface of the low stair-walls carved in bas-relief with a long procession of citizens from all parts of the empire, bringing gifts and tribute, climbing the stairs beside you or waiting at your side to go up: Elamites, Scythians, Phoenicians, Ethiopians, Indians and many, many more — each in his native dress and wearing his hair in the style of the time, leading his horse or camel, a pair of rams; holding out jars and boxes and lengths of cloth, two men carrying small and snarling lion cubs in their arms. Each group is escorted by a Persian or a Mede (Persian noblemen or guards alternating with Medes), the details of faces and curls, helmets and clothing crisp and clean in the radiant sun as if only just completed. Where the emperor is shown — and it isn't often — he is inside a doorway, walking along, followed by attendants with a fly whisk and an umbrella; on the stairs to the dining hall, servants with a napkin over one arm are bringing food and drink.

What kind of sculpture is this for an emperor's palace — that doesn't exalt any heroes or exist only for artistic or decorative reasons, but is itself a tribute to those bringing tribute? Every figure is treated by the sculptor with the same respect, even affection. Only someone with a gracious heart and eye — a natural loving-kindness — could have seen that clearly the inner quality of the different races and nationalities, given them equal dignity and at the same time made them so human and so communicative. For right through, the processions are laced with gestures of amity — a figure turning to speak to the man behind him, two holding hands, a hand laid on a shoulder or raised to the lips in greeting as if blowing a kiss; they even seem to contemplate each other as we did in the Shiraz Bazaar. It is one continuous and moving celebration of men trying to relate to the otherness of foreigners, of the brotherhood and equal rights of man, just as the whole spirit of this human-feeling place is that of a balanced, harmonious, self-confident age.

Sir Kenneth Clark, in his great commentary on Civilisation, named confidence as a quality absolutely essential to its existence. Does the omnipresent sun god, Ahura Mazda, spreading its wings in protection and glory over every part of Persepolis, have something to do with the confidence here? Or was it the ancient Persian's rational and generous faith in man? "God's plan for the earth is not turmoil but peace . . ." Whatever the cause, something remarkable happened here twenty-five centuries ago at what has been called the most sacred spot in Persia.

A work of art may catch a moment in time, like the figures on Keats's Grecian urn — catch it and preserve its immediacy forever. At Persepolis, the events, feelings, attitudes are not only arrested — they seem to be still going forward, as if that great procession were winding into the future, as if it were *still happening*. And it feels more than just Persian. Wandering about in the furnace of midmorning among those silent presences, those symbols risen out of lives lived in the desert, battles against drought — a thousand conditions unlike those we know — was to feel how at the deepest level of being, we, and they who created them draw, and are drawn from, the same source, like the water table under the earth. Our own attempts to portray brotherhood on post-office and courthouse walls are only a much younger, still hopeful version of what the people here did two and a half millennia earlier. What was beautiful was that the idea had been born, and that there are places on earth where the past is still this alive.

A MUSIC OF COLORS

TWO DAYS LATER, we were in Isfahan, in the extravagant Arabian Nights splendor of the Shah Abbas Hotel, walking across floors islanded with magnificent rugs, under ceilings glittering with colored mirror inlay of flowering branches, peacocks and gazelles. Thousands of artisans had worked around the clock in shifts for two and a half years to redecorate the original caravanserai as a palace, now partly owned by the Shah himself, yet when we rang for servants no one came for half an hour, and dinner — ordered from a two-foot menu and wretchedly served in a din of jazz — was worse than boarding school on the cook's night off. To regain sanity, we walked out afterward into the garden, once the courtyard of the inn and now a dream of blue-tiled pools and fountains, paths bordered by enormous roses and lined with rows of little quivering aspen trees.

The night was most curious, the first part of it as noisy as one might expect from being in a room over the front entrance on a busy street, then, sometime after midnight, so quiet that the stillness was almost palpable — the vast inflow of a new, dominating element. Sunk in it, asleep for I could not tell how long, I rose to the surface as if called and lay listening — unbelieving at first, then increasingly attentive, drawn steadily along on the unmistakable notes of an animal's call — the eerie and repeated "song" of a wolf. Here I should explain that in the weeks preceding our departure we had listened several evenings to an extraordinary recording of the calls of wolves, just released and made possible by newly sophisticated recording equipment; my ears were thoroughly attuned to the voices of wolves. I tried valiantly to rationalize this voice into the middle-of-the-night howling of a big dog, say a German shepherd, but it wouldn't work: quite simply I knew that it wasn't. Whatever the explanation could be — pet wolf or nearby zoo — the song was exhilarating, even in an odd way, comforting. The next disturbance was not, when the stillness was ripped apart by a hissing and roaring, the air filled with a choking chemical odor as the whole length of a wall across the street was spray-painted by powerful air compressors. In the morning, I asked our bright and charming young university guide about the wolf song. He didn't bat an eye; there were indeed wolves in the mountains around the city, he said, and in the intense quiet of the desert one might easily hear a wolf as being much nearer than it actually was.

The desert around Isfahan is more bleak, more absolute than around Shiraz, though in contrast to a certain cozy provincialism of the smaller city, Isfahan has the presence and authority of a great capital — which for many hundreds of years it was. It is also more of an oasis, with wider, shadier boulevards, even a river. This, the Zaindeh Rud, flows along under two highly ornamental bridges — all arches and pillars and galleries and bays — remarkably like the elaborate structures we built as children out of stone blocks. The city has many such fanciful buildings: palaces with exaggeratedly tall

and slender columns duplicated in long pools; halls and courtyards with delicate exuberance of detail; mosques whose
interiors are like jeweled caves. Through the streets streams
the twentieth century — noisy, smelly, oppressively startling
to anyone on foot and almost totally surrounding these islands
and coves of imaginative creativity and loveliness. So far, the
Maidan — seven times the size of the Piazza San Marco in
Venice and with a flowery and watery park down its full
length — is still uncluttered by cars and, incredibly for its
size, has the grace of old Persian miniatures. According to
some architects the most beautiful square in the world, it has
been used, rather like the Colosseum in Rome, for just about
everything, including polo and many other sporting events,
one of which was a contest between horsemen shooting
backward with bow and arrow at a golden bowl. The reflecting pools were empty when we were there, as they were
being cleaned of debris before being refilled for the celebrations; full, they must reflect the Maidan's unique unity of
architecture, its lovely proportions and harmony, accented in
the middle of one side by the Ali Qapu palace, at the ends by
two huge mosques and — final touch of genius — the much
smaller and subtle Lutfullah Mosque, off-center and refresh-
ing as the note or chord in a musical composition which is not
at all what the ear was expecting.

The Royal, or Shah, Mosque is surely one of the most
beautiful buildings in existence. Collection of buildings
would be a better term, since the main prayer hall with its
great dome and twin minarets is flanked by three vaulted
iwans, or porches, two other minarets, some smaller prayer
halls and courtyards and galleries — all entered from the
square through an eighty-foot-high entrance porch. At first

sight of the central building, dramatically set at forty-five degrees to the entrance and come upon without warning through a soaring archway, I was stung to tears and could not move, overwhelmed as I had been as a young girl on being led with closed eyes into the interior of Chartres and then, in the middle of the nave, opening them. "The buildings *float!*" one of our companions burst out, for although their mass and majesty dwarf a human figure, every surface — rounded, concave or flat — glistens or glows with such luminous brilliance, the proportions are such, that the whole effect is of lightness, airiness, space. Vaults and arches soar even higher, or so it seems, than the heights of cathedrals; the colors — turquoise, lapis lazuli, golden yellow, clear green and white combine in the mosaic and ceramic tiles into stunning or ravishingly tender harmonies. "It is a music of color," said our young guide. Above a dado of plain, tawny marble, every square foot is covered with endlessly varying designs that appear to dance and at the same time be at rest.

> . . . *at the still point, there the dance is,*
>
> . . . .
>
> . . . *Neither movement from nor towards,*
> *Neither ascent nor decline. Except for the point, the still point,*
> *There would be no dance, and there is only the dance . . .*

Walking slowly past and watching the subtle changes, it was as though I saw, really saw, design for the first time. Since childhood I had shied away from "decoration" and ornament, made vaguely uncomfortable by them — perhaps because of the Victorian clutter of many old houses I knew — and preferring plain and simple surfaces. Where had I been? What hadn't I missed? This was like going from Gregorian plainchant into the middle of a Stravinsky symphony, from an open lawn into the sun-dapple and leaf-stir of a midsummer wood. It was being introduced to a whole new language, a new experience of the senses. And more than the senses: what was most moving of all was that in its unfamiliar idiom the Royal Mosque felt just as holy, as filled with the splendor of the ineffable, as any of the great cathedrals of the Christian tradition, the impulse sprung from the same center, the same reality. It was a gigantic hymn to God.

Occasionally the impulse even found similar expression and looking up into the height of a vault or soffit, into the zenith of a dome, one finds a many-petaled, lacy design almost identical to that of Gothic rose windows. All other decoration is different: with the advent of Islam it was forbidden to depict any representational beings or objects — human or animal figures, flowers, leaves or incidents from holy writ. Religious and artistic fervor was driven underground but burst out in another form: all that repressed exuberance danced into swirls and arabesques and orchestrations of color, contriving here and there to depict ingeniously concealed flowers and vines, even fish, but mostly transcending representation altogether. Except for the Koran: this, like a deep obbligato of cellos and bass viols, surrounds whole prayer halls, arches over openings and underlines the exquisite openwork tiles which let the daylight in through doubled walls of domes in a glory of patterned light and shadow like sunlight through foliage. The scripture — wherever we saw it — was always in white on a deep blue ground, the beautifully ornate script sometimes spread out and stately as the adagio movement of a symphony, at other times delicate and attenuated as grace notes on muted strings. Impossible for us to realize what that writing looks like to the Moslem, or what kind of message it conveys. Does it say anything like: "Who shall not fear thee, O Lord, and glorify thy name? for thou only art holy: for all nations shall come and worship before thee . . ."?

Intoxicated as if given a new sense, we returned to the mosque at different times of day to absorb its brilliance and majesty, to rest in its flowery side courtyards. Exhilarated and dazzled, we then went around the Maidan and into the delicious contrast of the smaller, darker Lutfullah mosque — a quiet forest glade, peaceful and cool with intricately filtered daylight sparkling on the underside of the canopied dome.

When perception expands, everything around takes on a new appearance. I had never responded, for instance, to Oriental carpets and wondered what my parents saw in them, so as a rebellious bride I bought the plainest (and dullest) broadloom. Now, I studied carpet designs as if moving through exotic new landscapes and was mesmerized watching a village girl making one on the family loom. Her village, random as the tunneled habitat of prairie dogs, was a huddle of buildings around filthy courtyards through which wandered scrawny poultry and goats and runny-nosed children, yet there she sat in her dim room, fingers dancing over the rich earth colors, tying knots and clipping them precisely with flying motions of a knife. Such glowing loveliness to come out of that setting!

In the blinding desolation of the desert around the village, huge dovecotes stood here and there like the keeps of medieval castles; inside them collected the pigeon manure which gives Persian melons their wonderful flavor, Persian roses

their opulent splendor. Otherwise it was a country of stone,
its sparse life sustained by the hidden *qanats* tunneling under
its surface. The far-off green, the rounded domes and minarets of Isfahan looked, from there, like a vision.

The last afternoon in Isfahan, before returning to Tehran
on an evening flight, I came in from browsing alone in the
bazaar and walked out into the garden of the hotel. Surprisingly, no one else was there. It was just twilight; that radiance typical of southern latitudes — opalescence tinged with
violet — still lit the sky; the simple and lovely hanging lan-
terns along the paths were already lit. Over the rooftops to
the west loomed the sapphire dome of the Madrasseh Mader-i-
Shah, the theological seminary, between its two utterly phallic minarets; from one of them the muezzin was sounding.
The city beyond the walls made a subdued buzzing, less a
sound than the sense you sometimes have of the surge of your
own blood. In the half light, the crowds of roses looked
almost luminous; they overflowed with fragrance. It was one
of those rare moments when everything around connects and
falls into place like a resolving chord; a few moments later it
was dark.

We had heard that this would be the first night of the
illuminations and the boulevard leading out of the Tehran
airport was glorious. Arched over with light, it was quite
clear of traffic, but from where it joined a main highway until
we eventually reached our hotel was a traffic nightmare
which made a joke out of any other bumper-to-bumper jam I
have ever been in, and stretched an eighteen-minute drive out
to an hour and a half. What must have been the entire three
and a half million population was not only in the streets but in
motor vehicles, and not just automobiles but motorcycles,

trucks, buses and rattling old jalopies — anything on wheels that would move. Overhead shone canopies of light, festoons and fountains of light, peacocks with every eye of their spread tails a light, scrolls and arabesques and trees of light but almost no one was looking at them: all were too busy. Every avenue and street and alley was jammed solid and, unlike other such congestions, here there were vicious turmoils inside the crush: drivers simply refused to stand still, and if there were a few feet, a few inches of space in which to maneuver, they forced and barged their way through, yelling and challenging and cursing. Motorcycles with whole families aboard threaded between cars, tiny, large-eyed children clutching the waist of a child in front; cars fought for lanes and for any slightest advantage; our own driver brushed too close to a truck and blithely scraped the whole side of it — neither he nor the other driver even bothering to exchange a word.

Yet it was only an extreme example of what is happening wherever there are automobiles: take to the wheel and people's natures change as abruptly as chameleons, moved from grass to stone, go dark and gray. Motorists looking one another over from their individual armored isolation even resemble chameleons: the same careful, deliberate turn of head, the cold reptilian eye.

Over a late cup of tea in our room, I picked up the newspaper with the Empress's beautiful, serene face looking out from the front page and read her wish for her country: "to safeguard its culture and civilization from the negative effects of the industrialized West."

Isn't it possible to resist the automobile? Is our destiny, perhaps including an apocalypse, to come via four motor-driven wheels instead of the four horsemen? What are we doing to ourselves?

In contrast, on our last evening in Iran, we wandered into an idyllic example of human beings enjoying themslves humanly. Tehran is filled with parks, and one, the little three-acre Pahlevi Park, was a few blocks from our hotel. Entering it was like coming into a delightful garden party; it was a model of what a park can be. Crowded with people — whole families, students, lovers, the old — still, all their different interests were cared for, with quiet retreats for reading or intimate talk, malls for strolling, playgrounds. Nowhere was there any litter and the beautiful willows and cypresses, the perfect and untrampled turf was straight out of Persian prints. Here and there were benches but mostly people sat along the seat-height stone edging of lawns raised above the level of the walks. Guards and attendants were about but weren't officious and in the playgrounds they helped to keep the children moving on the slides and gently reproved or shunted aside those children who were monopolizing play equipment. Best of all was the water — fountains and pools of it and, following the length of the park, a watercourse descending in a series of steps and falls in which children dabbled and waded and floated small boats. In the holiday dusk (it was the birthday of the twelfth Imam), with colored lights going on, glowing and shimmering in pools and fountains, it was a beautiful and heartening little fairy tale of a scene.

Four years before this, the man who was to become head of the United States Environmental Protection Agency said thoughtfully that the time was coming when people wouldn't be *able* to get to beaches and recreation areas anymore: there

would be too many cars. We have so much to find out and
learn, he said, about what people really need for recreation;
how best to utilize living space and, most important, what
kind of immediate environment people must have in order to
be happy. Grass, moving water, trees — and companionship:
Omar Khayyam had suggested it, just as Saadi told us that if
some men are badly off, the whole of mankind suffers. I felt
ready to leave Iran; I also felt that this ancient meeting place
of peoples, from Persepolis to three acres in a modern, traffic-
tortured metropolis, had much to tell us.

KABUL

FLYING EAST out of Tehran was like crossing a threshold, and once past Mount Demavend, its serene Fujiyama form dusted with pink from the sunrise, what remained of the Western world dropped away. Each hour of desert unrolling below put it farther behind and roiled the unearthly landscape into more extreme contortions, swirls, pinnacles and, finally, waves of mountains. I seem to remember that after the first fifteen minutes of flying there were no visible human settlements of any kind. Except for the plane in which we sat and the globally similar rituals of air travel, everything European had vanished; we were making the leap from the Near East into Asia proper, where only the thinnest shell of accommodations and a sparse net of familiar advertising separate the traveler from a world totally strange to him.

As we stepped out into the brisk air of higher altitudes and drove into Kabul, the greater foreignness of people's faces and dress was immediately striking. The men wore baggy pants and colorful embroidered vests; they tied their turbans in elaborate twists with one long end left trailing. There were few women about and most of these floated past in *chaderis*, finely pleated silk garments which cover them completely, raying out from a snug little cap with a mesh "window" through which the wearer peers. Enchantingly feminine clothing, though a little spooky: who is inside that soft cloud of periwinkle blue, chestnut brown or dark green? Is she young, old, pretty or plain? To men she must be a tantalizing figure. At the doorway of a mud-brick house, she lifts the front of her silky cage and throws it back over her head as she enters — too late for her face to be seen.

Leaving Tehran, I had asked one of our party who had been in Kabul before if there would be bad traffic — I still quaked from that monstrous jam — and he burst into laughter. A few camels, he replied, and a bus or two — which was only a slight exaggeration. In the broad paved streets of the modern part of town, shepherds were walking in the October sunshine with their herds, stopping under a tree to knock off a few dusty, yellowing leaves for their creatures to eat — the first hint of the country's aridity. In the center of town were more animals — mostly donkeys loaded with fruit and produce or almost invisible under mountains of straw — and more people, including barefoot men, usually in pairs, who pulled carts loaded with tile, pipe and bricks by means of wide forehead straps rigged back to the shafts. I remembered that my uncle, living in China as he did, abhorred the use of rickshaws — the indignity to the men as well as the terrible physical strain — and I wondered whether the fact that these men pulled building materials and not other, more privileged humans made any difference. They looked vigorous and healthy; at a red light (these exist in Kabul, too) they chatted and laughed. There were a few motor vehicles — trucks and buses, but what buses! Every square inch covered with painted scenes framed in arabesques and curlycues — the Taj Mahal (many of these), flower gardens, fountains, faces, peacocks — the coloration full of vivid turquoise and sharp pinks.

Having had to get up at 2:45 A.M. for the flight, we spent the afternoon of our arrival on the balcony of our hotel room. It is wonderful after a jet flight to be able to just sit — sit and contemplate the new where-you-are and slowly resume the lost sense of reality. Contact with the earth, sitting out on rocks or grass, is even better — as if one absorbed from the ground messages of location and once again reconnected.

From the hilltop hotel we looked out over the city, spread among tawny fields and circled by barren, rock-scarred mountains, which recede, plane after heightening plane, into the Hindu Kush, toward Iran, toward Russia and China — the farthest, highest ranges so little more substantial than sky that it took field glasses to verify their presence. Miles away on the far side of the valley, a reddish haze in the air, an occasional plume of dust indicated the airport and arriving or departing planes. Nearer, on our side, the mud-brick blocks of the old city clung to the side of a steep hill, like nests of mud wasps, their light-and-shadow scenery being shifted all afternoon by the sun. The contrasts, in that high, clear air, were sharp and violent; the fact that the temperature may vary fifty degrees between the two sides of the street no longer seemed incredible.

But it was the people in the near view who, without knowing they did so, and not even aware of being watched, restored us from a succession of traveler's disappointments, annoyances and hurryings: an old shepherd who was following the random grazing of four sheep up and down the small hills of a vineyard; a woman following, sweeping up the sheep's droppings and collecting them in a sack, pausing to do some kind of handwork when the animals didn't move on; a student, or maybe he was an actor, walking slowly along the road right below us, reciting out loud, an open book in his hand and an elegant full-length coat of striped silk swinging as he walked. People kept appearing and reappearing on the wide S-loops of the hillside road, even though it seemed to lead nowhere in particular and was just a pleasant place to walk.

The air grew cool; in steady modulation the mountains went from gold to orange, to rose and mauve; the far, insubstantial ones flared up like blown embers and died suddenly into dusk. From around a bend in the darkening road came a piped tune, very gradually growing louder and nearer, fading out at a bend or the interruption of a wall. Finally it came clear as five young men strolled by, one of them playing on a flute, and with great musicality, an intricate and lovely melody. No one hurried or talked loudly; at another curve in the road the group melted out of sight and hearing, to return much later, the flute still playing, in the dark.

Human figures in a landscape are always strangely appealing, as the old Chinese and Italian masters of painting knew well, but it was the pace of these people we watched that healed like the laying on of hands: that ambling and strolling — to the grazing of sheep, the sounds of words or flute — were all to the rhythms of breath and heartbeat and to something more interior still. The afternoon, neither long- nor short-feeling, was timeless: we existed in it, were nourished by it, like the sheep in the green vineyard.

What one is to make of this in the way we live in developed, industrialized societies, I am sure I don't know. Perhaps only that intervals of quietly looking, and listening, and not *doing* much of anything are far more important to our sense of being and of meaning than we realize, and that they are possible almost anywhere. I remembered on that afternoon in Kabul a similar occasion, when three of us of like mind sat on a rock looking out over a wild northern valley, speaking of this and that out of long, comfortable silences. In its cool evergreen freshness, that place was the very opposite of this, yet there, too, we had been at a still center, as connected to the oriole flashing in and out of a tree, the ringing sound made by a halyard slapping a nearby flagpole, as the hub of a wheel is connected to its turning rim. New impressions streaming in have a way of stretching out the sense of time passing, so that whatever the age of the body, one perceives like a child, but these afternoons I tell of are of a different order — they are, or feel, out of the stream of passing time altogether and in some simple and familiar place one had thought forever lost.

In the animal market next morning, held in a big open space in town beside the dwindled-to-a-trickle river, we were returned to a scene unchanged for hundreds if not thousands of years. Acres of men and boys with their beasts were gathered: clusters of donkeys, sheep, camels, goats and fine Arab horses, while huddles of men bargained and made deals, then led away the animals of their choice — the broad-tailed sheep with their terribly queer "bustles," weighing thirty or forty pounds, daubed with brilliant dyes in the wool to distinguish ownership. Some of the haggling was alarmingly tense; in one group two men were laying violent hands on a third, forcing him down in the dust, pressing on his shoulders; in many faces there was an aggressive intensity more controlled and therefore more menacing than the excited behavior of southern Europeans. No women in sight, though I thought I saw one peer from a dirty tent pitched near the highway, and little girls as well as small boys were scurrying about collecting the animals' droppings as eagerly as if they were coins — putting them into round straw trays or gathering them up in their skirts and running off with them. We drew stares and second looks, sometimes collected onlookers. One of our party had camel dung thrown at her (it missed), and a piece of melon rind, thrown by some children, hit me. Other children were charming, particularly one handsome boy of eleven or twelve who had great presence, authority and warmth. An outstanding person, yet I believe it was he who, with smiling eyes, took the big shears in his hands and mimed cutting off our noses with it to the onlookers' silent appreciation — and it wasn't quite all in fun. There was rock in these people, like the outcroppings of their mountains.

What faces they have — living bequests of every invasion! In that one crowd, as throughout the time we were in Afghanistan, we saw pure Mongols, left behind by Genghis Khan — some with typically Chinese droopy mustaches and thin little beards; pure Jewish (believed to be descendants of one of the lost tribes of Israel); Arab; Persian; some almost African — more in color than in features though I noticed a few strongly resembling Masai; here and there a blue-eyed Caucasian; Greek, left behind by Alexander the Great's invasion, many Indians. There didn't seem to be any such thing as "pure Afghan," unless they are the outstanding men with aquiline noses and fearless good looks, but all have the same ruddy warmth to their skins, the proud, aloof glance. They impress one as strong, self-reliant people of great ruggedness — as they must be to have overcome the obstacles of harsh, unforgiving land crossed and recrossed in both directions by the peoples of Asia and Europe. The astonishing thing is that with all that cross-pollenization of genes each strain has remained so conspicuously itself.

Be careful about photographing their women, we were warned: foreigners have had stones thrown at them for that. Which perversely brought to mind images of the undressed women in our ads; what would, or will, the Afghan man think of those? Since Amyas thought he could manage photographing by spending enough time in a crowd somewhere, he and I went to the bazaar. It was unbelievably crowded and smelly, wildly interesting. Laden donkeys, herded sheep pressed along beside us. Meat vendors spread their ghastly joints and shreds of unidentifiable this-and-that on the pavement where flies covered them in buzzing, iridescent hordes. Men sold beads and necklaces and lengths of wool, furs and embroidered sheepskin coats; a man beside whom we perched on a wall sharpened wicked-looking knives; vendors were selling a sticky confection like a large cube of peanut brittle; and children wove in and out holding live chickens by the legs. Once, while Amyas was off photographing somewhere, I was silently watched, gazed at, by a very tall Mongol, maybe a Buzkashi rider from the country around Mazar-i-Sharif, for he wore a rope over one shoulder and tied down around the waist as they do. The look was so totally closed, I found it rather sinister, yet after passing him I couldn't resist a look back: he was still standing there unmoving, looking at me, no expression whatever in his flat face, his almond eyes.

For the first and only time in Kabul, that afternoon we passed close to the women in *chaderis*, and with the sun full on their mesh windows I found I could make out their eyes, glinting a little, like water at the bottom of a well. I tried smiling. Amazing: something came back through that screen — a sort of sparkle or ripple to show that they smiled, too. One woman's eyes really danced and shone as I smiled at her. Impossible to know whether it was with pleasure, amusement or derision yet I felt that great sense of exhilaration one gets in faraway places when a human connection, however tenuous, has been made across every kind of gap.

VALLEY OF THE BUDDHAS

BECAUSE OF SHORTNESS OF TIME and the vagaries of local flight schedules, we made only one long trip away from Kabul — to Bamiyan, oasis valley in the middle of the Hindu Kush. Before the sea lanes diverted cargo away from routes overland, this was an important stopping place for caravans to and from India. But Bamiyan was also, and for many hundreds of years, a great center of culture and religion, particularly Buddhism, brought there by missionaries, who probably came because of one remarkable man, Kanishka, ruler of the Kushan empire. A patron of religion and the arts, his empire stretched from Benares to the Gobi Desert; his winter capital, Peshawar, was the gateway to India. An historian writes that "for the first time the Hindu Kush [which means Hindu Killer] ceased to stand as a dividing line and became a veritable vortex instead." Dynasties, invaders and caravans came and went; foreign influences which had begun with Alexander's occupation of the valley left traces of their arts: Greek, Sassanian, Gupta, eventually Islamic. For a thousand of these years, Buddhism flourished in the valley and pilgrims walked from as far away as China to visit and marvel at the colossal statues of Buddha sculptured out of the cliffs. Finally it was destroyed by Genghis Khan who, it is said, never meant to go there and sent a young grandson in his place to besiege the valley's fortress. When the boy was killed, Genghis was so devastated by grief he came himself and saw to it that every man, woman, child and animal living in the valley was put to death. Hundreds of years later, nomads sheltered in the caves the monks had inhabited, and villages gradually returned, but Bamiyan's great days were over until in our time archaeologists discovered its treasures.

One third of Afghanistan's population of nine million is still nomadic, and half an hour's drive out of Kabul we met a large caravan. We were northbound toward the route through the mountains, they were going south toward warmer latitudes. Stopped beside the road, we watched them pass: one man on foot at the head, then the lead camel carrying a huge black iron brazier (the hearth!), followed by a string of camels bearing quilts and cook pots, tentpoles and the black goats'-wool tents in tight folds — all shambling along with aloof, bored faces, bells jingling around their necks. Babies and small children rode in nests of quilts, long poles tied on like railings to keep them from falling off; a matriarchal figure rode a donkey and kept saluting with hand to her lips, exactly the same gesture as that made by figures in the frieze at Persepolis. Several baby camels padded beside their bed-slippered mothers and one scruffy-looking dog limped along in the middle; everyone who could do so, walked. Up and down the line, however, rode one man on horseback, hawk-nosed, handsome, with piercing eyes and proud expression — probably the leader of the clan. My eye caught his; he kept looking and so did I until his horse had passed out of range. My look must have shown my interest and curiosity, my admiration of his fine masculine bearing. What his showed I

was not sure — curiosity, yes; and a certain dominating arro-
gance. The women gave the opposite impression from that of
the mysterious tented creatures in the capital; they carried
themselves proudly, even defiantly, and wore their brilliant
skirts and shawls and jewels with flair; they looked at us
openly, some with warmth, others with a definite challenge.

The whole slow and purposeful procession set up waves in
me I couldn't account for. I suppose I am as susceptible as the
next person to the lure of gypsies and the nomadic life, and as
a child I had an almost classic encounter when I came, alone,
on a gypsy camp in the woods near our rented summer cot-
tage. Their looks and faces, the colorful dirty wagon and
black cookpot hanging over a fire fascinated, repelled and
frightened me all at once; for a long time afterward they
appeared in my dreams. But this meeting on a road in
Afghanistan stirred something that felt very different and
much deeper than any "raggle-taggle gypsies" nostalgia, as
though the earliest struggles for existence in harsh and hostile
country, the seasonal migrations in search of warmth and
food, had left their traces in my own unconscious, went back
perhaps to a time that predated agricultural man when there
were only nomadic tribes wandering the earth. In the still
mountain air, the caravan passed almost soundlessly with only
the shuffle and jingling made by the camels, the creak of their
loads and the staccato hoofbeats of the leader's horse, yet in
the few minutes it took them to go by I knew more certainly
than I had ever known the reality of something nonpersonal
or "collective" in the unconscious — as real as the physical
residues of our biological history. Yet recognizing this
atavistic "memory," how did I, coming from my part of the
world, connect *here?* Was it possibly because of my Danish

mother's ancestry? My father, teasing, used to tell me that a certain look at the corner of my eyes, a width of cheekbone, probably came from Swedish blood (mixed into most Danes far back), and therefore from the *Huns!* he would add triumphantly, with his heartiest laugh. The caravan dwindled away, we drove on. And I wondered: is it possible that *all* of us on earth are connected and had the same early history?

Once out of the Kabul valley with its paved road, the long hard drive began. The awfulness of that dirt road into the mountains would be hard to exaggerate — its hundreds of curves, potholes, precipices, dust and always (so it seemed) at the most difficult places, encounters with one of the incredible buses — decorated and dirty, stuffed with people, animals, bundles till the inside could hold no more, the roof so top-heavy with overflow it was a marvel they didn't go careening off at every curve. For roughly a hundred miles this road climbs between high, bare mountains of ever-changing colors — sulfur yellow and orange, violet, slate blue — all dry, dry, dry. Life clings to the river at the bottom and to the narrow strip of terraced and cultivated land on either side, no more than two fields wide.

Over and over on this journey and not just on the one drive, it was water that was the central theme; a single thread, it ran through everywhere we went: water — or its absence. In Iran it had been the pearl of great price, strung (invisibly) along the *qanats* whose dry craters beaded the deserts for miles, and in Shiraz the spring beside which the poet Saadi lies buried is almost as important a shrine as the carved alabaster bier, but in Afghanistan water seemed virtually nonexistent; there can't be many regions in the world more arid and dusty, made of more rock and sand. Flying into Kabul from Iran,

you see along the narrow valley bottoms the tentative green
of a line of fields, a few trees; the mountainsides, if you look
very closely, are hazed over with a mist of green, giving them
not the color itself but a hint of it — like the iridescence of
certain fabrics where one thread of a special color among
many others shows itself in a particular slant of light. Flying
at much lower altitudes, as we did on returning from
Bamiyan, we saw the mud geometries of small settlements in
the most unlikely, lonely and steep valleys, some almost at
snow line in the Koh-i-Baba range, their one reason for existence a thread of water or the flat eye of a tiny pond, its
outlet carefully guided and cajoled in ditches down to one or
two fields, a stand of a few aspen trees, brilliant gold in the
October sun. The nomads must pasture their goats on that
hint of green, milk serving as liquid when there is no water,
their flocks doing for them what irrigation and farming does
for the settled people. The bare mountains, right up to ten
and eleven thousand feet, are veined and webbed with the
tracks of their caravans, moving up in the spring and down in
the fall to warmer altitudes and somewhat better grazing.

As we climbed up the hundred-mile-long valley, the stream
that glittered among glittering aspens on one side of the
wretched road or the other, or burbled down a raised ditch
beside us, grew constantly narrower. Abrupty, at a check-
point where we stopped to fill our radiator before the Shibar
Pass, the last vestige of it vanished. We climbed out of the
valley into high fields scratched with ploughing, over the
eleven-thousand-foot giddy-making top, which is the water-
shed of the Indus and Oxus river basins, and down into a
formidable gorge which nearly closes in overhead between

overhanging cliffs and holds, suspended, rocks as big as six-story buildings — as precariously balanced as if a giant squatted there holding them, barely keeping them from pounding down onto anyone mad enough to traverse such a place. The gray stream bed was bare rock; it flows only in spring. No habitation, not even a caravan in transit. Finally, in late afternoon, the Bamiyan valley and water again, glimmering along over stones and nourishing fields and pastures, growing avenues of hundred-foot trees. Families were out harvesting potatoes, bullocks were ploughing and cattle wandered about drinking out of roadside ditches filled with fast-flowing water. We had returned to life.

Visitors to Bamiyan stay at its one hotel, on a high plateau across the valley from the long cliff peppered with openings and with the two niches in which stand the giant figures of Buddha. Behind the cliff the Hindu Kush rises to sixteen thousand feet. Guests are usually accommodated in *yurts* — a kind of round tent of wicker and felt, lived in by northern tribes and adapted here for tourists' comfort — but because of an overflow of visitors we were in the main building. Our room with its one window facing the view had two iron camp beds with a blanket each, three nails from which to hang clothes, a single chair and a single bare light bulb hung from the high ceiling. *Bath!* proudly announced the boy who brought up the bags and, bending over double, I followed him through an opening into a cavelike place where besides toilet and basin there was an oil hot-water heater. It was a monster — gulping fuel, stinking of kerosene, making weird knocks and belches. We'll have to turn that thing off, we said. Half an hour, many trips up and downstairs and much sign language later, this had been done but nothing could stop the slow black leak across the gritty floor, the evil smell which was to companion us all that night.

We sat down on the two camp beds and looked at each other. Amyas said he was cold and put on a heavy sweater; a few minutes later he was having a teeth-rattling chill. I wrapped him in both blankets and took his temperature: nearly 104 degrees — the highest fever he had had in the more than forty years we have been married. Amazingly, an American doctor was discovered among the overflow of guests but except for the fever he could find nothing wrong and assumed it must be a twenty-four-hour grippe. We spent a weird and troubled night; the patient groaned with miseries he could neither identify nor explain and I was frightened yet trying not to show it, also trying to keep warm, for by morning the temperature was in the thirties. Several times I looked out of the window: the stars were enormous; the Buddhas, hooded with dark in their niches, stood impassive and austere.

The doctor had been right. By morning, weak but recovered, the patient wanted a big breakfast and afterward went down to the terrace; at noon we drove over to the cliffs.

Though severely damaged, the two figures in their unmistakably Greek draperies, one of them a hundred and twenty, the other a hundred and seventy-five feet high, are deeply awesome. Almost as much so is the labyrinth of galleries, assembly halls, sanctuaries and cells for a thousand monks which honeycomb the pinkish rock with openings for nearly a mile: religion relegated to a womb of rock where it was safe from attack for many hundreds of years. The worst destruction occurred with the influx of idol-smashing Islam but such important frescoes and art work as remained have been removed to the Kabul Museum. Tribesmen have inhabited the caves and in the summers, now, hippies have lived in them; roofs and walls are black with soot. Still there are many tantalizing remnants of paintings to be seen: arching over the head of the smaller Buddha, a Sun God stands on his chariot in a costume like that of the early Persian kings, surrounded by seated and haloed Buddhas; the head of the great Buddha is circled by crowds of male and female divinities — Buddhas and bodhisattvas purely Indian in feeling, worldly female figures with nude breasts and cymbals in their hands and one figure of a man wearing the long belted tunic and fur leggings of central Asia. A pair of gentle dovelike birds stand facing one another, holding between them in their beaks a string of pearls; ribbons and foliate scrolls flutter and twine, the colors remarkably like those of Pompeii which, since the Kushans had embassies to Rome and brought back artists, isn't too surprising.

There wasn't time and Amyas wasn't well enough to explore the interiors but in the noon hour we spent there we were almost alone before the hundreds of mute openings, the strange presences of the towering, nearly faceless colossi. No people were living inside, we were told, but in several places we heard the moaning and murmuring of doves, enlarged by a grotto's vaulting. A haunted, haunting place — made more so by the memory of the night and, months later, by a curiously related fact. Before leaving home, Amyas had spent some days with his older brother, fatally ill with cancer. Both of them knew that it was probably their last time together; the family agreed that though they would cable us we should under no condition return. When we arrived in Nepal, letters told us of his death (the cable never arrived): he had died the day we went to Bamiyan. Not till long after we got home did I learn that the hour of his death, allowing for the time difference, was exactly when Amyas had been shaken by that chill. Maybe it was "only" coincidence (though coincidences are vastly stranger than we are ready to admit) yet it is now forever inseparable from the great mountain Buddhas, the starlit silence of that valley which has seen so much life, so much death.

THE ROYAL BUZKASHI

As WE FLEW back over the mountains to Kabul, every fold and color and detail clear and the sun still high, it seemed impossible that part of the Hindu Kush was blotted out by a dark haze — not clouds, but the arrival of impenetrable dusk. Fog? Here? No, sand. Such clouds of it, ours was the last flight out for the next two days.

Around A.D. 400, the Chinese monk Fa Hsien wrote of his visit to Bamiyan: "The country is in the midst of the Onion range. The snow rests on them both winter and summer. There are also among them venomous dragons, which, when provoked, spit forth poisonous winds, and cause showers of snow and storms of sand and gravel. Not one in ten thousand of those who encounter these dangers escapes with his life." Poisonous winds . . . today there are new breeds of dragons around, but for the next few days we experienced storms of sand, fortunately not gravel, although sometimes it felt like that. Two days were really "foggy" and several times, out of a blue sky, sandstorms blew up. They were quite horrifying — like blizzards obscuring everything, closing in more and more closely, driving against you. The dusk was falling quickly and quite early now: at five the light faded and half an hour later it was almost dark. On the "overcast" (as the paper called them) afternoons, the sun became veiled even earlier and the air and sky looked like a wintry, snowy afternoon at home.

One of these afternoons was spent in the Museum, much of the time in the Bamiyan Room; though even without one's having been to Bamiyan, the Museum's small and unique collection would be enthralling for its jewels of Greek, Buddhist, Indian and Islamic art. Waves of migration, conquest, trade tossed these up here in fantastic incongruity: an austere head of Buddha and a sophisticated Indian tree fairy carved in wood; a highly detailed ivory throne and one of the earliest known sculptures — no more than an oval pebble but with the features of a face cut into it at such an angle that it has the natural perspective of a face seen three-quarters view. The only known representation of the great Pharos of Alexandria is also there, on an amazing example of early glass: a vase ten or twelve inches high so skillfully made that several full-relief boats — skiffs with fishermen sitting in them — float around the sides. Has any Venetian glassblower excelled it? And one little room, we discovered, contains nothing but portrait heads surprisingly like those in medieval cloisters and cathedral doorways: realistic, profane, grotesque — yet these date from the third and fourth centuries instead of the thirteenth and fourteenth. Did some migratory wave bring their kind to Europe? Or do the same forms tend to develop, at different periods, in different parts of the world? Whether because of the comfortably assimilable size of the various collections, or the sharply clear vignettes of the ancient world which these exhibits evoke, one receives a more intimate sense of the timeless, universal urge to create than one usually gets in large and overwhelming museums. Shells on a beach, these relics: some fractured and tide-worn, others shiningly perfect, the life that informed them long gone yet also — and one prays, indestructibly — *there*.

(Half a year later, at a concert in New York, while I was totally absorbed in Strauss's tone poem *Death and Transfiguration*, images of these objects I describe appeared in my mind for no clear reason. How to explain such visitations? Like wild ducks planing in to land on a pond, they were there, vital and vivid, and for a little while floated easily on the rippled surface of my attention until the music once more took over and, without my noticing when it happened, were gone.)

In contrast to these remnants as the sea is to its beach treasures, the Buzkashi is the past alive. Ancient sport, originated no one knows when, it has been played by competing teams of horsemen on the northern steppes for hundreds of years. Sport? Fray seems a more appropriate word. There are a few rules, particularly the one time a year it is played in Kabul, on the king's birthday — "the Royal Buzkashi" — but on the vast plains of Balkh and Jozjan and Samangan where neither the number of horsemen or the area of the "field" (which may extend clear over the horizon) is fixed, it must be the wildest kind of encounter.

The name means "dragging the goat" though it is often, and as we saw it, played with the carcass of a calf which has been beheaded, eviscerated and toughened by soaking in brine. The object is to gather the carcass up from a starting circle on the ground, ride away with it and around flags at the end of the field and drop it in a scoring circle — opponents meanwhile blocking, intercepting, pursuing. Teammates help one another out by passing the calf to a rider in a better

position or by running interference, and the horses themselves — all stallions — after years of training and experience,
press every advantage by shoving, battering, standing braced
or racing free, if necessary without any message from the
reins if a rider is taken up with securing the calf under one
thigh or riding out of the saddle, hanging on to his horse's
side, even under its belly, to escape the whip of an opponent.

There is a theory that the game grew out of the raids of
Genghis and Tamerlane, when invading Mongolian horsemen
descended on nomadic encampments, scooping up animals as
they rode, and were then pursued. Long before that, the
horsemen of Central Asia had been famous; they gave Alexander the toughest resistance he met, and one theory has it
that the returning Greek soldiers' tales of their riding created
the legend of the Centaur. Perhaps it was the other way
around: in the minds of men watching the first wild horses
streaming across the plains grew the longing and symbol of
half man, half horse which, in time, became almost flesh and
fact.

On the king's birthday the Buzkashi takes place ten miles
south of Kabul on a field 450 by 350 meters which lies between two small hills — the one to the east with a very old-
looking village along its ridge, and a higher one to the west
where women are allowed to sit and watch the contest from
at least a quarter of a mile away. Along the western edge of
the field are canopied grandstands for tourists and notables,
separated from the action by a sort of dry moat and now for
the first time a wall, since the previous year horses had crossed
the moat, knocked over tent poles and the canvas collapsed on
the spectators. At the middle of the field and in front of the

starting circle stands the royal pavilion, striped red and white, decked out with masses of flowers and furnished with Louis XV style armchairs.

With the games due to start at two, all the roads were closed at one o'clock to let the royal party through; we were instructed to get there before noon. If the crown prince (whose father was at Persepolis) hadn't been half an hour late, the time would have felt short, there was so much to look at. Long before anything began to happen, crowds were arriving on foot, on horses and donkeys, and people collected on the rooftops of the ancient village. The pavilions and flags and, a little distance away, a collection of brick kilns, shaped exactly like the tournament tents of old paintings and tapestries, gave the scene a wonderfully medieval quality; when a row of mounted lancers rode onto the field — each carrying a flag on a tall, tall staff — and arranged themselves at intervals around the perimeter, we were in the Middle Ages.

Out on the field, onlookers wandered in the noonday heat and the umpires (former players, or *chapandoz*) rode about in magnificent striped-silk coats, their horses caparisoned with ornate fabrics, some shining with silver bridles and ornaments. Each stallion to be ridden was attended by his own *syce*, or groom, who stood holding him or walking him slowly; the animals were very quiet and calm though it was startling to be actually brushed by one walking by. They were already saddled, the saddles — deeper than our western ones — lined with rich carpeting. On the ground, the *chapandoz* sat around in small groups, waiting: huge men, most of them, with huge hands; dressed in heavily quilted jackets, high boots like our own cowboys' but with a more extreme, tucked-under heel, and little round fur caps with a different kind of fur as the rim. Each team wore a different-color jacket, some with an insignia crudely made out of cloth tacked onto it: the outline of a goat, a rose, a crest. All the players had the same impassive faces and acted oblivious to stares and clicking cameras; considering the violence and risks they had ahead of them, their indifference seemed magnificently arrogant.

A few police captains appeared, then troops of them — helmeted and wearing a kind of battle dress — and little by little, with greatest difficulty, they cleared the dry moat and the wall of the people that had occupied them. All around the field the crowd of standees grew and thickened into a tensely waiting wall of male humanity; the suspense was almost palpable. With the onlookers arranged, the police — only a few by now — settled themselves at strategic points and out on the field one *chapandoz* after another mounted: his *syce* adjusted the stirrups, and the riders, at a slow, slow pace assembled into teams and rode to the far side of the field, facing the stands. Fascinating to watch the legs of ten or more horses walking in close grouping: a kind of beautiful impressionist abstract of walking — as though it were one body being transported on all those swinging stalks. Now the eight teams formed themselves into one long line facing the stands, somewhere between eighty and a hundred horses and riders, divided into groups of olive green, sand beige, scarlet, royal blue, black, midnight blue, tobacco and dark brown.

They waited. In place well before the scheduled two o'clock start, they were kept by the crown prince's lateness for more than half an hour, standing perfectly motionless. Meanwhile the carcass was brought in and dropped in the starting circle, a black hulk weighing over a hundred pounds, to be fought over for the rest of the afternoon; the tension was screwed up another notch.

At last the royal party arrived, a fanfare of trumpets sounded and the line of horses advanced — in such controlled unison and so slowly it was hard to perceive the actual movement toward the royal tent — the umpires in their glorious paraphernalia forming a smaller line in front. Every man bowed low to accept the royal salute; the first two teams to play (last year's champions and this year's challengers), stayed forward as the others withdrew to the sidelines, and at the shot of a pistol the Buzkashi began.

Impossible at first to see what was going on: twenty horses milled in toward the black mass of the calf — pushing, shoving, colliding, rearing, and the calf would appear to be lifted only to fall back again in a roil of dust. Hard to understand how a *chapandoz* could ever get it off the ground and get free in that mess, yet we learned later that teammates shove others off to let a rider through and that the rope I had seen on mens' shoulders in the bazaar is used to hook themselves to the pommel. The first match was a particularly closed-in one, the contest extra hard-fought by both champions and challengers, but once a horseman did get away with the calf there was no holding him until riders from the other team charged in or caught up with him, yelling and flailing with their whips, hitting both their own horses and their opponents'. Sometimes two horsemen thundered along side by side, the calf tucked under the leg of one, the other rider all but out of his saddle trying to wrest it away. The horses — either very big or surprisingly small and agile, but all powerfully built and with unusually heavy legs — glistened with sweat yet didn't lather; their sides heaved with hard breathing, they were almost constantly in the thick of action though occasionally a rider appeared deliberately to rest his mount by hanging back for a few moments and letting the mad turmoil whirl on without him.

Some turmoils were heart-stopping. Three or four times during the matches, two horses in full gallop kept going perfectly straight, flat out, and right into the crowd of spectators at the side or corner of the field — strewing bystanders, knocking some over, tearing around behind the stands and reappearing on the field at the other end. Horrifying to see a body or two lying immobile after the fury had passed and then to see it moved onto a stretcher and into an ambulance. Ten were injured that afternoon, and one, a soldier guarding the crowd, was not expected to live: he didn't get out of the way fast enough and was actually trampled.

One player (the word seems a travesty) was thrown and broke his leg; later, another disappeared from view, with his horse, right into the middle of a galloping melee, stood up, his arm broken, and the horse — a beautiful palomino — righted, shook itself like a wet dog and trotted away. A third also went down with his horse and must have been kicked in the head. He stood up, looking utterly dazed, blood trickling from his forehead and staggered forward and around like a drunk, looking helplessly up as if asking directions from the sky. The fray boiled away and left him behind; the horse, on its feet again, went off by itself; without further ado the rider collapsed in a heap and an ambulance drove up and took him and one of the injured bystanders away together.

I had been somewhat prepared and braced for all this, expecting from what I had read about the Buzkashi to be appalled. You may have to look away, one man had told me beforehand. I didn't. And we stayed for three out of four matches, enthralled by the excitement of the most gripping spectacle we had ever watched, with its dramatic backdrop of mountains, its atmosphere of a medieval tournament. Why we were both so deeply stirred was less understandable. Men got hurt, were cut by whips; opened their jackets to the waist, baring huge wet chests; horses heaved with exertion and galloped back into the melee. Though I'd started the day still weak from a sharp attack of the Afghan variety of tourist distress (like everything in that country more violent than elsewhere), I was restored and invigorated by something profound and even cleansing — as the violence of Greek tragedy is cleansing. No worse (except for the inexcusable lack of protection of those bystanders) than rodeos in which men are gravely injured, nor as shocking as a steeplechase I was taken to as a young girl when a rider, crowded by others, rode head on into the colossal trunk of an oak near where we stood, and one heard the cracking of bones and, a few minutes later, the crack of the pistol which dispatched the horse. I nearly fainted on that occasion and was laid out on the grass; don't stand at all well the sight of suffering, least of all that of animals, usually inflicted as it is by us or our machines. "The most revolting spectacle I ever saw," said one fellow American of the Buzkashi as we were walking away from the grandstand, and in a way she was right.

What *is* it? I asked Amyas (and myself), that evening and for several days afterward, wanting to understand its meaning, wondering if the violence out there on the field reflected hidden violence in me. It was the purest kind of contest for one thing, he thought — of men, horses, skill, speed — and not, we agreed, an exploitation of animals as in bullfighting for instance.

Long afterward I was thinking about that rugged land, which has been stormed over and laid waste by armies and by goats, eroded by drought; where the past persists in the faces and fortitude of the people — as in their shrewdness and ruthlessness; where closeness to the earth and conservation of everything that will help life along in the harshest of environments is everywhere evident. On this battleground of attackers and resisters, aridity and the extracting of water, I saw that the Buzkashi *is* that contest, in the flesh and ritualized. And at the most primitive, deepest level, it is a primal drama: like their Mongolian forebears, those riders on their stallions were making the wildest efforts, half out of the saddle, horses rearing around them, to seize food or defend it from seizure. That was why one could accept the injuries and the blood: we were back in the past of the human race, in a part of the psyche as primitive and powerful as raging hunger. The horsemen of the Buzkashi reenact the struggle of life to survive.

In retrospect, the most upsetting event of that afternoon was a fight which broke out in our grandstand between two tourists apparently over nothing of consequence. A punch was thrown, glasses knocked off and the two men, one attacking, the other reeling backward, staggered past us until a policeman separated them and with an arm laid around the victim's shoulders led him away, blindly hunting in the gravel for his broken spectacles. It was naked hostility and is the harshest memory of the day — as the most sorrowful one of that proud land is the dust we raised in the faces of people along the road to Bamiyan. Plodding along the narrow track with their donkeys or camels, they would step out of the way to let us pass, holding a turban end across mouth and nose, no sign of annoyance or impatience about them. I hated, each time, the affront of the automobile to man and his animals. Western inventiveness was degrading an ancient partnership, smothering them with its defiant indifference.

THE VALE OF KASHMIR

THE NAME is a caress. Try to say it fast — it isn't possible.
A romantic-sounding place with an odd assortment of associations: houseboats and mountains, kingfishers; fine woolen
shawls one's grandmother wore and one's mother draped over
the grand piano; lakes with reflections; water — always
water. They all fit and it's true: a visit there is a lyric of
gentleness and liquidity. Some gardens actually do float and
the farming is luxuriant and moist — agriculture lifted out of
water, encircled and enriched by it. The houseboats are
childrens' fantasies of the Ark, doodled over with decorative
carving, while other boats glide through acres of lotus leaves
— veined green bowls four feet across in which a drop of
water from a paddle rolls back and forth like a silvered glass
bead and which, in spring, harbor the flowers sacred to
Buddha. How can there be a populated part of the earth
today in which one feels so little discord and appearances have
such clear and primal innocence? Only two hundred miles
from the Khyber Pass, gateway to Afghanistan, it is an opposite world — and a world of opposites. But it doesn't disclose
itself at once. There are discrepancies to be resolved, gaps in
oneself to be faced and, in our case, the transition to India to
be made in between.

A third of the way from Kabul to New Delhi the remarkable shift begins from stark mountains and deep valleys to the great green plain of the subcontinent, apparently stretching away forever and scattered over its surface with some of the five hundred thousand villages of India — no longer the blond mud blocks of the desert but clusters of brown roofs. Dirt roads, pale in the surrounding green, converge on them from many directions; seen from the air, the villages resemble darkhubbed wheels laid out on the patterned plain, which is dotted with separate trees standing in pools of darker green shade. After so much rock and sand, the eye drinks the sight gratefully.

But few cities can be harder to arrive at than New Delhi. The bureaucratic airport procedures, with triplicate forms to be filled out and exasperating scrutiny of documents to be endured, are a caricature of British punctiliousness; driving into the city a nightmare of two worlds. Cows saunter about or just stand and moon; oxcarts have to be slowed down for and gone around, as well as thousands of bicyclists and little high carriages crammed with large families and each clattering behind a trotting horse — every variation of speed and obstacle to be negotiated, accompanied by continual hornblowing.

The once-famous hotel in old Delhi suffered from similar disharmonies. The powerful air conditioning made it so cold and draughty we moved our beds into the middle of the room and pulled the sheets over our heads, while the stately old four-bladed cooling fans still hung from the high ceiling, unusable. Because of so much new machinery about, windows which overlooked trees and lawns had been refitted with frosted glass or covered over altogether: you couldn't see out. Soft-spoken, gentle-eyed houseboys were plentiful, and helpful, but in the dining room we couldn't hear one another for the piped-in music.

Feeling as though our minds and senses had been whirled in a blender, we went out for a sunset stroll and straight into the fantasies of a Rousseau painting. From palms and banyan trees came raucous bird-talk and the flash of parakeets; one tree was clotted with buzzards and whole families of monkeys prowled, or ran, tails high, around the vine-tangled arches of a ruin — while a toucan, with his monstrous bill, eyed us malevolently. Dizzily, I felt returned to Africa and, what with the streets of dilapidated buildings and rows of new villas we had been driven through, a hodgepodge of Africa, Korfu and Florida suburbs. Not till we drove back to the airport at sunrise and up the Raj Path — magnificent, wide, stately — past Government House and the vice-president's home with their Sikh guards immobile as copper statues, did I believe I was in the capital of India.

The Vale of Kashmir . . . it didn't seem possible but from the air it looked dismal, and *dry*. And the airport at Srinagar was an armed camp full of gun emplacements hidden in haystacks and masses of soldiers with stern expressions on their faces. Stiffly starched and pleated frills fanned straight up from their tightly wound turbans, front to back like a cock's comb. The image of a rooster crowing from the top of a barnyard manure heap, neck thrust forward, wattles and comb-points shaking, flew into my mind. Imposing and resplendent creature, unaware of his own absurdity.

It is dangerous to have preconceptions of places, there's such a screen to be shredded away before one can really perceive. Also, the tourist's first views of Dal Lake are incongruous. All those houseboats a few feet apart and advertising their names and owners in large signs — Shalimar, Golden Gem, Kashmir Palace — fancied up with intricate porches and gimcrackery yet with a slightly down-at-heel look, make it a kind of floating Oak Bluffs, Massachusetts, or the midway of a British seaside resort. Although the keen disappointment of the first hours quickly softened, it recurred each evening when the electricity failed just when it was most needed, as at every contrast between the exaggerated advertising and the reality, the pathetic claims of the chief houseboy and his over-humble servility. Then, one morning, as I sat up on the roof of our houseboat, the screen dissolved like sunrise mist; I was no longer someone observing the surrounding scene: I was inside it, or rather, it was inside me.

On a little pier running out from a shack, probably belonging to one of our servants, two children squatted, bathing their ducks. One after another they brought them out and, holding them by the wings, dunked them up and down in the weedy water. Beyond, at the edge of a raised field, a man irrigated his crop with a big bowl-bucket on the end of a counterweighted sweep. Down went the bucket, coming up again full; at the edge of the land he rolled it gently over with his bare toes, to spill its load. The rig squeaked a little, adding to the symphony of sounds: dipping paddles, people's voices, bulbul songs like drops of water, hawk cries; duck quacks, some like laughter, others the most ribald protest. There were percussive wood-knockings from boats, autumn insect chirrings, laundry being slapped; very rarely and far off, an automobile horn but never any generalized background sound — only the waves made by living spreading outward in the still, still air.

This total lack of wind gives the lake much of its charm and interest, makes the surface of the water a reflecting glass of boats, figures, feathery poplars, mountains — the Kara-koram, when we were there, already covered with snow. It allows the harmony of sounds, even acting as their sounding board. At sunrise it collects the mist, at dusk, the smoke of all the evening cook-fires. Perhaps the extreme reflecting power of wind-free water is what gives the light its magic: a kind of pervading brightness which is at the same time tender. Seated in it, out in the little garden beside the boat, our friends' leaf-shadowed faces took on a lovely radiance.

All morning, out in the open water, the "village" life pro-ceeded, the native boats, *shikharas,* floated past on their reflec-tions. Those taking passengers had tipped-up awnings of gaudy chintz under which passengers reclined on mattresses (above them a sign: FULLY SPRUNG), while a boatman paddled behind them in the stern. Open ones — very long and pointed bow and stern — carried peddlers of fruit and vegetables, flowers and tourist attractions; there was a drug-store boat and one for postcards — dreadful, out-of-focus pictures grimy with handling — a *shikhara* loaded with furs and one with nothing but knives and nutcrackers. A little out of the main thoroughfare two men stood twirling long poles as if winding spaghetti on a fork, the boat slowly filling with wet, rich weeds off the lake bottom which would be used for composting the fields. In another, two men paddled to a certain point, laid down their paddles and in perfectly syn-chronized motions dipped two large nets into the lake and hauled them up, shaking out the water. Very quickly they fingered the weeds, throwing out as they searched, scooping up a few tiny fish from each load. Baitfish, as they showed us, hanging a vibrating inch of silver from a line weighted with a stone. They smiled at us appealingly, souls in their eyes. The blades of their paddles were the shape of hearts.

On the Sunday afternoon we were driven — it was too far to go by boat — to the Moghul Gardens, Nishat Bagh and Shalimar, where George, a scientist and the pragmatist of our party, said he fully expected to see a pair of white, plaster-of-Paris hands materialize in the air as he arrived. We laughed at that so sentimental song where there is no body, only pale hands — but none of us knew until we were there that the gardens were the gift of Shah Jehan to his beloved, to whom he later erected the Taj Mahal. They are very beautiful with their background of steep mountains and outlook over the lake, their ancient chinar trees like gigantic sycamores, the masses of lovingly cared-for flowers. But the long pools had only a skin of water in the bottoms, a trickle dribbling out of rows of spouts which should have made a fine and gushing display. It being a holiday, many people were about, mostly well-to-do Indians who strolled through the gardens looking and enjoying. A few groups, sitting on the lawns, played cards; one had just finished tea and two beguiling-looking young Chinese girls were washing cups and saucers in a brook. Scarlet, purple, saffron, apricot-colored saris moved among the borders like larger flowers. The women wore diamonds in their nostrils and one, right out of a Rajput painting, had glitter on her eyelids as well as her clothes.

But I was not happy about my ineptitude in relating to the Indians. They irritated me. Our chief houseboy's servility and cringing appeals rubbed me exactly the opposite way from his intentions, or what I supposed them to be. Our drivers, who wandered over the road like sacred cows and even rounded curves on the wrong side or risked neck and limb to pass a bus in order to tail another car, drove me into panic and shouts of NO! Don't DO that! Very different with people I only looked at or had eye language with, like the enchanting pair of women, one nursing a child, who sat on the curb outside the New Delhi airport when we arrived there. I smiled at them and they responded; the young mother lifted her child to look at me and be looked at; when our car finally left — after incomprehensible discussions, arguments, delays — they waved and waved and the baby's hand was held up, to, to wave goodbye.

Incomprehensible is the key word. Everyone on earth should have one other, world-used language. Not only did we have the screen between us of alien customs, religions, history, but we didn't even have the opportunity to experience the screen. It was a double ignorance. Add to that the bewildering Indian pronunciation of English and the soft voices that often have no carrying power, or timbre, and it wasn't surprising that we mutually ended in thickets of non-understanding, from which we — and perhaps they, too — emerged frustrated and angry.

With the merchants of Srinagar it was another matter. The unqualified perfection of what they handled — wool so fine they drew fifteen yards of it through a woman's ring, embroideries delicious as confections, boxes snapped open to disclose, in delicate gold settings, softly shining topazes and Kashmir sapphires, rubies and spinels (their paler relations), amethysts, moss-dark jade — all this gave them the assurance and suavity that come from knowing that what you have is the finest there is. They were in a position to learn other languages and customs, could afford to serve cardamom tea brewed in a samovar brought into the showroom, and expect customers to find their way there in the first place by walking through an alley mounded and splattered with excrement.

In the cooperative carpet "factory," where two hundred families worked at their own pace (children coming in afternoons for a couple of hours after school), a whole family might be working at the same loom, one member — often an eight-to-ten-year-old boy — calling the pattern, which was worked out in a code on slips of paper stuck in the warp. The instructions, echoed each time by "Ha!" (yes) from the others, merged into a sort of chant which sounded merrily, almost musically, in the high airy shed through which birds flew. In a neighboring shed, carpets were washed and the water squeezed out with long hoes — also to singing. It was a cheerful place. Beyond, lay the Jhelum River which bisects the city, clogged with native houseboats and, on this branch, with floating chinar logs. Ducks and geese sported in the filthy water; women hung out washing or spread chilis to dry. On one boat a woman vomited into the river while her neighbor, a few yards downstream of her, dipped in a cup and drank from it. Along both banks was the typical concretion of ramshackle medieval-looking houses with overhanging upper stories, balconies, half-timbered walls — as if they had been piled up in some crazy game until they became top-heavy and appeared ready to fall. But such beautiful objects, so much life as came out of that accumulated filth and decay! Like the enormous Persian roses and melons fertilized by centuries of pigeon droppings. Like the glittering scarab beetle the ancient Egyptians revered, which hatches, feeds and reproduces in a little ball of dung.

Returned to our houseboat from these excursions, we were

back among familiar comforts and unfamiliar service, enjoying the kind of companionship impossible in hotel dining
rooms or the makeshift compromises of meals in bedrooms.
Sitting around the big table, faces lit by that radiance off the
water, or in the evening by the wildly fluctuating electricity,
we were relaxed and gay. George and his writer wife, Betty,
carried on a continuous but affectionate duel — she teasing
him about his scientific facts and anecdotes ("You're being a
bore again, George") and he — never without his two wrist-
watches, one set to local time, the other to Boston — teasing
her about her sometimes gross inaccuracies, for she was by
nature a storyteller and a dramatic one. Eleanor, the most
intellectual of us and the best informed about what we were
seeing, leaned forward eagerly, her head at a lovely angle on
her long neck, deeply involved in every discussion while
Henry, her husband — another practical man — quietly
chuckled and enjoyed steering us back onto the track. In
another houseboat, across the narrow garden in which we
gathered for tea, were the English couple who had arranged
the trip — John, who gave us history briefings and shep-
herded us through airports and arrivals, and the lovely, tire-
less Valerie — valiant Valerie as I came to think of her. With
them were "Freddy" and her husband, plus the eleventh
member of the party: Freddy's camera, which was always
"doing something peculiar," getting dropped or jammed, a
true enfant terrible. Elegantly dressed and coiffed Freddy,
with large dark brown eyes, getting on and off planes, into
and out of cars, carrying a black hatbox by a handle of orange
wool (it contained the felt hat her husband had worn in
London), was full of little stories and lighthearted com-
plaints — the most gallant of all of us and the most intrepid

traveler. In her wake followed round and cheerful Bill, who didn't care as much for all this moving around as she did but did it for her sake. Impeccably dressed (the seersucker suit appearing the day we flew to New Delhi), loving his Maryland farm, its gardens and animals, he was a stranger in these strange lands yet he always communicated, with smiles and pats of affection, a squeeze of the hand — like the touching figures in Darius's frieze.

The next to the last day, Amyas and I, with two paddlers and the boy Gulam, who was bright and spoke fair English, went for a long *shikhara* trip through the farm country. Five minutes out of our area, we were on a canal which wound through farms and settlements and past temples out into quiet open stretches of lotus gardens. To the eye there was nothing here but water and greenery — even the raised fields with their poplar hedges were divided by channels of water — but stop and listen and you heard voices from all around and discovered people were everywhere. Yet the most pervasive sight and sound were ducks: there must be a duck population in the hundreds of thousands. They are fed in the morning and let go; no one steals or kills another's ducks and at evening they return to their owners. All afternoon along the winding, watery way there was a continuous quacking, dabbling, darting about.

Behind us, our paddlers chattered in happy voices or sang — a song which they seemed to improvise, returning after long meanderings to the same refrain — yet when a kingfisher landed on a stalk, flashing and chirring, and Amyas carefully picked up his camera, there was immediate, utter silence, the paddles weren't allowed out of the water to drip. Boats slid past us loaded with vegetables or cuttings, often paddled by a child, alone, kneeling in the narrow bow. People were smiling, particularly the children who — it seemed everywhere we traveled — were the ones who want to communicate and who reach out; whatever it is that happens, it is only later that we grow wary as partly domesticated animals, or close up like flowers when daylight goes. Women paddling *shikharas,* wearing sunset pinks or dragonfly blue, floated like flowers on their reflections but, near to, turned shyly away or drew a corner of cloth across their faces. It was the children who leaned our way, hands raised and folded as in prayer; their sparkling eyes invited us, they smiled and called out *Salaam!*

One girl, about ten, had a radiance of eyes and face tender as sunlight through an April leaf. In the photograph she is quite plain but the animation and incandescence of her look will always remain with me. What will become of her? Will she spend her life in those watery gardens, working in the fields and bringing up babies, going home at dusk to one of the hundreds of houseboats we paddled past, the dark interior glinting with shiny pots and the light of a cook fire? She may not live to grow up: I watched another girl of her age come down to the water's edge, scoop some into her cupped hands and drink.

Daylight drained from the air around us and deepened on the mountains. Smoke began rising, straight and slow, from among the poplars and lights shone here and there. In a stand of chinars hundreds of birds collected, arriving in great flocks that argued with strident flowing voices before they settled down. In the thickening blue of evening woodsmoke we paddled home.

The last morning, like every other, a man's voice sang the

muezzin before there was any light at all. Not recorded or amplified as is usual now, but a wandering calling out, which was singular yet impersonal — a spark wavering upward from a campfire. I lay in the dark and listened. That wistful cadence, those foreign words were another solitary and groping attempt toward — what? Salvation? Understanding? It echoed everyone's struggle to absorb into himself, or transcend, all the terrible opposites of existence. At certain moments — "peak experiences" — of music, or loving, or communion with friends, we are given intimations that, in the words of the Abbess Juliana of Norwich, "all shall be well; all manner of things shall be well." We are reconciled. But are intimations enough? Until you can look into the eyes of your own child and accept the child drinking from the Jhelum, the eyes become skull holes in the living corpses at Auschwitz; or, at the very bottom of self, endure love fermenting into hate and the desire for violence, or watch hope reverse into despair and *still* feel that with all manner of things it is well — nothing is ever "enough." And in Asia the opposites to be absorbed are such as to stretch the heart to bursting.

The time grew near when we had to leave. Madam (said the houseboy Habib), no one wants to leave Kashmir. Madam, it is a paradise on earth. Habib's irascible, high-voiced boss, owner of the houseboats, picked and gave each of the ladies a flower. A *shikhara* brought the jeweler, who, like a conjuror pulling tricks out of a bag, delivered various satin and velvet boxes. Someone else, known only as Butterfly, brought other packages done up in glossy brown paper. Sitting out in the warming sun, we admired each others' scarfs and saris, the lamps the sun lighted inside the jewels.

At the airport were more soldiers, new precautions, and in

Amritsar, where there was a half-hour wait during which Amyas and I perched on a luggage cart in the shade of our plane's wing, fighter jets screamed overhead without a break; the border of West Pakistan was nine miles away. Five weeks later bombs fell where we had stood and the war had begun.

"Tell me something," a friend said later that winter when in Dacca men had been tortured to death before the crowd filling a sports stadium, "why is it that those most gentle people are also the most ferocious fighters, inflict the most horrible suffering and *tolerate* suffering as they do? Why?"

What could I say. What is the answer, except perhaps that extremes breed their opposites.

Houses of the Gods

THE ROAD TO KATHMANDU

ASIAN ART is full of cosmic symbolism, the kind of symbol which "brings man into communion with the powers of heaven," and one of the great themes is that of the mountain. In those ancient civilizations nothing had greater importance: the mountain was the supplier of water, therefore of life; it had access to heaven.

The whole of Nepal, its actual geography, can be seen as a cosmic symbol. A three-leveled figure, as composed as the meditating Buddha who was born there, its base rests in the green *Tarai* or jungle country; the uplands, particularly the valley of Kathmandu, form the fertile lap which sustains life; its head is the top of the world. Everest's native name is Chomolungma — "Goddess mother of the snows"; the Himalayas are symbolic as well as being the highest mountains on earth.

Hima is snow and *laya* a house: the Himalayas are the houses of gods yet those great presences feel more like actual deities. To get to them, or just to the uplands, used to take weeks of travel on foot or muleback; by car it is still a difficult two-day drive over a pass often closed by inclement weather. There is no railroad; shipments of goods are made over a cable strung overland on poles. Flying into Nepal is rather like flying to an island separated from the shores of the world by rings of mountains. One after another, going from west to east, the plane passes the icy giants with the names that sing: Dhaulagiri, Annapurna, Himal Ganesh, Himalchuli, Gauri Sankar; Sagarmatha, Lhotse and Makalu. A hundred and twenty miles farther, on the border of Sikkim, Kanchenjunga stands alone.

Somewhere in the last ten minutes before Kathmandu, the plane finds a gap in the foothills — they would be called mountains anywhere else — and threads through between the forested summits and ridges that shelter the valley farming. Below, and climbing far up the mountainsides, are terraces like the most beautiful sculpture, neither arbitrarily built up nor leveled off but carved and curved to follow exactly the natural contours of the land. At some points the passage is alarmingly narrow; mountainsides stream past, the valley floor rises to meet the incoming plane, then abruptly one is out — received in a welcoming, level lap. It is a kind of birth.

For me as for many travelers, just getting to Nepal, and before any meeting with the religious mysteries or the people, is to have a deep and unshakable sense of arrival — to feel: here is where all the paths of the earth and of my own being converge; this is where, without knowing it, I have been going all these years. For places, in the broadest sense of the word — landscapes, towns or entire countries — seem to echo different aspects of ourselves, as if they had their counterparts in consciousness. There are the places in which one feels so much at home they are like the rooms of childhood; and there are countries of the heart, as those of the Mediterranean are to the northern European; certain cities and their cultures which liberate and excite while others make for nothing but melancholy; demonic scenery as evil and oppressive as Blake's satanic mills. Do places, of themselves, mold our perception of them? Or does our consciousness make them what they are? Either way there is some deep inner correspondence.

In Nepal the correspondences were, for me, multiple; the land itself was wholly satisfying in an inevitable way. The valley of Kathmandu, or whatever it reflected in me — or both — felt as magic and harmonious as a mandala — that beautiful diagrammatic form that evolved, in Tibet, into such magnificent expressions. No wonder they originated in that part of the world. Other places have given me strong feelings of arrival — of "now I am there" — but in Nepal I had the further sense that here was the source of much of what we are — of our long love affair with the earth, which the heavens gave us, of our continuous dialogue with powers and realities we cannot see. And perhaps this sense of being in a cradle of humanity, between earth and heaven, was why, from the first day, time felt so different: seemed to extend outward without limit so that one lived at the center of it, unpressed.

From the windows of our room we stared, unbelieving, at the panorama of the Himalayas, spread out a full hundred and eighty degrees. In the noonday fields directly below us, people were working in lovely-to-watch rhythms at cutting and gathering rice; the dark roof-lines of the city beyond broke unexpectedly upward into the festive outlines of pagodas. To one side, a conical hill, standing alone and dotted with trees like a child's drawing, culminated in a temple with a gilded tower which had huge eyes painted on it and was crowned with a sort of Christmas tree ornament, which quivered and glinted in the sunlight. On either side of this, two identical structures with steep, rounded shapes duplicated precisely those of the distant peaks — so much more vertical and ridged with ice than other mountains are that they seem more like sculptural fantasies.

For in spite of all one has read and imagined about them, the Himalayas couldn't be more improbable. Our first day there, George, the physicist, drew diagrams for us on the back of the menu to explain how the snowy heights which appeared and vanished again in a clear sky from behind a near ridge were a mirage. Excitedly he'd burst out: "There! They're coming up — do you see them? That's the sun's heat on the ice fields, bending the light rays, like this . . . There! Now they've gone down again, see?" You don't argue such a point with an authority on light and spectroscopy, but I am still not decided whether it was mountains in mirage we saw, or clouds, or something else altogether. It really doesn't matter. What was very clear, however, that first week following the end of the monsoon season when the mountains reappeared from their months of hiding in cloud, was the extraordinary power of their presence. Fifty miles away, the row of highest peaks stood no taller in the intense blue, probably took up less sky than do the Swiss Alps, usually seen at closer range. What, then, made them so godlike? Why did they feel like more than magnificent scenery? The light on them — like the light in which the whole valley shone — was other-worldly; the air had a brilliance and clarity which, over much of the earth's surface, it is losing, but even at the two ends of the day or at the infrequent times when wandering clouds alternately concealed and revealed them, they made themselves felt with overwhelming, awe-inspiring majesty. Kathmandu residents may claim not to "notice the mountains much" (as one of them remarked to us) but there is no question that in Nepal as in the other mountain kingdoms — most of all Tibet — living in that company and at those altitudes makes for a naturally religious, worshipful and mystically inclined people. Going to Nepal is to go to an exhilarating mountain world; it is also to enter a world where religion is as vital as the air.

Like other visitors we were at once impressed by how gay and outgoing, how secure the Nepalese people are, and when I asked Carol Laise, our ambassador, to what she attributed this, she replied: "I think their deep-rootedness in religion — their faith — has a lot to do with it. It is a steadying, vital force in their lives and the continual festivals and celebrations and ceremonies give them much pleasure."

Our real introduction to Nepal was to attend a ceremony — one we had heard about beforehand and which, like the Buzkashi, we looked forward to with mixed and troubled feelings. Live sacrifices of animals; we were curious but the idea was repellent. Also, it happens that I'm not only fond of animals, I am convinced that they carry deep psychic importance for us, connecting us more than we know to ourselves, to our remote beginnings and to the unity of all life. I believe a fearful retribution is going to result from our drastic and irresponsible rupturing of that unity: that as more and more creatures disappear from the earth we will suffer a terrifying loss of our sense of humanity, our sense of self. And though this refers to "wildlife" rather than domesticated lives, still the whole way to Dakshinkali I dreaded what we were about to see.

As if smiling at such foreboding, the way was one continuous, joyous celebration of the earth at harvest time. The long side valley was filled with groups of people cutting and threshing rice, spreading the rice straw out on the ground to dry in precise, fan-shaped patterns; in the early, green-and-gold light the women, wearing rainbows of colors, were archetypal figures in the way they moved and smiled and swung the long sheaves of their hair. As part of the harvest festival, swings, twenty to thirty feet high, had been erected beside the road by tying together four upright stalks of bamboo (still leafed at the top) and children were swinging in them — in one, a lovely young girl, laughing at the sky, long hair flying. As we wound along a hillside hundreds of feet above a meandering river, the landscape arranged and re-arranged itself so that anywhere you looked a single wonderful tree, usually a bo tree with glittery leaves, stood right at the top of a little hill, against a snowpeak — somewhere where its accent was beautiful. Streams coming down from the mountains raced under the road, shrines stood beside it; there were no villages but many scattered or loosely grouped thatched-roof houses the color of a robin's breast in spring.

When not distracted by this visual feast, I talked with our guide about religion. Madhu Sharma was an unusual young man, a graduate student in political science at the University; we came to know one another well and to become good friends. His vocabulary, articulateness and clarity of expla-nation were exceptional, his curious Indian accent and intona-tion frustrating, as it was with everyone we met, yet one never felt embarrassed asking him to repeat something. I asked him that morning if he was a Hindu and while not answering this directly his reply was typical of the open-minded Hindu view that "there are many paths to the top of the mountain." He believed, he said, that there were many aspects of the one Creative Principle and many approaches to it — that no one religion had an exclusive priority. "I take what seems meaningful to me from several." He had a fine grasp of the complexities of religious expression that we saw while we were there and a sensitive way of explaining them, also a detachment from opinion which was rather Buddhist. Often he would say: "I don't *know* about this, but it seems to me that . . ." or "One explanation of this is . . . another is so-and-so." A handsome, slight man with curly hair, wonderful eyes and an outgoing, affectionate nature, he was unusually light-skinned so that except for the eyes he might have been an Italian or a Greek.

We talked about the goddess Kālī, whose shrine we were about to visit and where the sacrifices were to be made. Consort of Shiva — one of the trinity of chief Hindu deities in a vast pantheon — this negative and destructive aspect of the Divine Mother, the female energy of the universe, Kālī usually appears as a fearsome creature girdled with skulls and brandishing a sword, her face the image of violent ferocity. The Hindu gods and their icons are full of paradoxes, however, and this representation of the Mother Goddess "as the tomb as well as the womb of all life" symbolizes the mysterious concept that destruction and production originate from the same source — are two sides of one another. Also, though I already knew something about Eastern religions, I was to learn an idea new to me: that the destroying god may destroy what is, to our minds, evil and not just what is "good." It was a further revelation of how deeply indoctrinated we Westerners are with the sharp division between good and bad, heaven and hell, body and spirit — all the "opposites"; with no connection between them in the mind, the very word "destructive" automatically and instantly signals "bad." Yet Shiva, the Destroyer, is the destroyer of death, and of time. Good? Bad? Only in a cosmic view larger than is conceivable to our limited, self-attached minds can these distinctions we make be absorbed and transcended. We are a long way from being that developed.

As we entered the mountain gorge which holds the shrine, Madhu explained that there was a double purpose to what we were going to see: the animals were sacrificed to the goddess with a supplication and the food enjoyed afterward in an atmosphere of celebration, either at home with a party or here, near the shrine, where there were outdoor ovens and tables. It is a very pretty place for a picnic, he added. Still dubious, I felt somewhat better on hearing this; at least the animals weren't wasted, or left on an altar for the buzzards.

The long flights of stone steps leading to the bottom of the gorge were crowded with people — holy men and beggars and, along one side, vendors of articles to offer Kālī. Arranged on the round straw trays used for winnowing grain were flowers, eggs, bowls of rice — each tray a still life composed as if by a painter; trays holding pots of powdered pigments — saffron, vermilion, indigo, kohl — were like painters' palettes. In the crowd streaming down the steps with us, people cradled a duck or chicken in their arms, or were leading a kid whose horns had been painted a brilliant color.

It is a holiday kind of place, teeming with action and festivity. A little river rushes through, bouncing down under big trees in a series of falls and pools, making a joyful sound. From above, the shrine is barely visible for the glitter of light on leaves and water, but there is smoke rising from it and a denser crowd and after a last long flight of steps you are there. Outside the high grille fence which surrounds the sanctuary, sandalwood burns in a row of shallow pans, giving off a delicious fragrance. On a stairway rising beyond the shrine, bells ring off and on quite continuously — audible punctuation to the ceremonies proceeding below. It is hard to see these fully for the crush of people entering and making their supplication at an altar, handing over their offering to one of the two priests dressed in blood-stained white garments. Men, women, children, all crowd through and wait their turn, faces intent and reverent, women in their best saris, the men in native dress, some in clean white shirts and pressed trousers. Fruit and vegetables, eggs, even a handful of flowers are presented. An animal is given to the priest and a big knife wielded — very quickly and skillfully for there is never an outcry. A chicken's body is tossed into a narrow trench between the outer fence and a wide stone block so that it can't flop about, the head handed back to the donor for offering to the goddess.

The day we were there, no one seemed to mind our presence, our wide-eyed staring; people went about their business, serious and purposeful yet in a festive mood. I stopped to admire a particularly beautiful baby, blue eye shadow making her enormous eyes even more so, a little cloth-of-gold bonnet on her head, and the mother, who had her at breast, was warm and responsive and held the child out for me to see better. Later, the grandfather was holding the sleeping baby and he, too, greeted me with nods and smiles, but in general no one paid the slightest attention to us.

I made myself watch as carefully and detachedly as possible

the killing of a little black kid, its fur wet with holy water. The head came off at one blow and the priest held the neck over a cup to catch the first blood, then held it for a few moments over a stone gutter, or groove, which was steadily running blood. The head, lovely with its painted horns, was treated in a special manner — decorated with flowers and, I thought, incense burned on it, before it was laid on the altar. Later, the body was taken down to a big pool below the shrine where, along with other creatures, it was first dipped in the water, then eviscerated and the viscera carefully washed and cleaned; after which it was dipped in a huge caldron of boiling water and the fur scraped off. By that time it was ready for cooking.

As with the Buzkashi, I couldn't believe my lack of recoil until it came over me that this was ritual killing and, if you eat meat at all, had much more dignity, even compassion, than the process in our vast commercial slaughterhouses ending with cellophane-wrapped cuts on the supermarket counter. Here, the animal to be sacrificed was at least honored, the killing done swiftly and mercifully and the creature's death celebrated with ritual — ringing of bells, burning of incense on its brow, collecting the first blood — while its preparation for cooking was a community enterprise, shared with others gathered around the mountain pool and the steaming caldron.

Some extremely primitive region of being must be stirred by the sight, waking racial memories of great occasions when creatures were offered up and eaten in propitiation or gratefulness after near starvation, perhaps simply to celebrate. I was reminded of Ruth Sasaki, the remarkable American Buddhist who had her own temple outside Kyoto, and her telling us of the Buddhist's feeling that every meal is a kind of sacrament; how it is possible, and desirable, to feel that whatever is eaten has given its substance — its life — for one's benefit. Far from being shocking and revolting or just a curiosity, Dakshinkali remains in memory as a quite holy place.

Walking back up the long steps, sadly shaking my head at cripples and importunate, begging children, the sense of ceremony we were leaving behind gave me a lonely feeling: in our world ceremony has so dwindled away and many great and small occasions, relating to the seasons of the earth and of ourselves, go by either unobserved or degraded by commercialism and triviality. That the instinct for ceremony isn't dead but has been suffocated — from within, by the vacuum of exhausted myths and, from outside, by the claptrap of a culture of things instead of people — seems evident in the spontaneous creating of ceremonies in the counterculture. Young people making their own ceremonies of marriage and birth strike me as one of the beautiful things happening in the ugliness of today's world. Without any sign as yet of the spring of new meaning, they scorn outworn rituals as if they were badly preserved flowers and they ridicule imitations; the plastic bouquet with an artificial scent can damn well stay in the florist's window! Yet aren't formal observances and collective gestures natural to the race? A bird breaks its neck on the picture window and the children lay it out in a box with ferns and flowers and give it a burial; lovers celebrate their private anniversaries. What is new — or perhaps a replay of the times in history when meanings were dying — is the individual creation of ceremony instead of accepting a dictated one — the substitution of the intentional for the traditional. When established authorities and institutions fail, we start over again, like children, with the entire past in our blood, the present as open as a new day.

TEMPLES AND DEITIES

KATHMANDU has two satellite cities: Badgaon, about nine miles to the south and Pathān, three miles away and across the river; both cities were once capitals of the kingdom. The center of each, particularly Pathān, is a constellation of temples, shrines, gold statues of kings on top of carved pillars, and stone statues in the middle of the street, niches holding figures of deities, and pagodas — every square inch of their supporting beams and rafters carved and gilded, or painted with engagingly naïve erotic subjects — the edges of each successive roof hung with a row of metal dangles, which glint in the sunlight and tinkle in the wind. On every old building, however plain, the balconies, doorways and window frames are of intricately carved dark wood, wildly imaginative in design so that from one window of the palace in Badgaon, for instance, the king — or was it his wives? — looked out through the fanned vanes and "eyes" of a peacock's outspread tail. All these wonders stand as close together as the monuments of the Roman Forum must have done but, being on so much smaller a scale, are even more concentrated. An outdoor museum, its displays are just beginning to be known and studied; it will take years and years before they are catalogued.

In the middle of this wealth, ordinary living goes on and there are crowds of people and animals, wandering chickens and goats. Women sit gossiping on a temple ledge, while right under the eyes of a meditating king a mother shampoos her little girl's hair and a goat rests in the shade, leaning against a statue of Garuda, the half-eagle, half-human vehicle of the god Vishnu. Skeins of smoke from a food stall drift among temple pillars; the air is redolent with odors of cooking and feces, spices and grains.

It being harvest time, large areas of pavement were completely covered with grain drying in the sun, which from time to time someone came and turned with a shovel or furrowed with a bare foot. In one place, surrounded by golden brown rice (and most unusual outside a shrine) a stone lingam, the phallus of Shiva, stood circled by the *Yuni* — their combined forms of creativity and fertility representing the Creative Force of the Universe. A man stood there, praying: "He is worshiping the Great God," murmured our elderly, pious driver.

Right beside the brooding white dome of Budanathstupa, a little way outside the city, we watched a woman toss shovelfuls of rice into the air while a group of women around her, acting with the precision of dancers, waved straw trays to winnow the grain of chaff and dust. Overhead, lines of prayer flags strung from the steeple down to rooftops gave the place the air of a holiday-dressed ship and from a temple came a stunning sound of drums and chanting punctuated by loud clashes that trailed off into the rustling chatter of barely touched cymbals: harvest rites, religious celebration, prayers — all intertwined.

To someone coming from a part of the world where there

is no living mythology, where the meaning of traditional religion is fading or obscure and the evidences of it mostly restricted to the interiors of a limited number of buildings, it is overwhelming to be this abruptly and densely surrounded by religious myth and symbol and ceremony. It makes you feel as one supposes explorers do on coming from wilderness or desert into a community teeming with people or as, after the near-lifelessness and loneliness of New England woods one is set down in the Serengeti among those hundreds of thousands of creatures streaming across the plains. Often, at first, I felt bombarded as if by a babel of meaningless sounds and came away fascinated but hopelessly confused. What was sacred? What meanings did these things hold for the Nepalese? Which temple was Buddhist and which Hindu? It was enlightening to learn from an American Jesuit scholar, who was writing the history of Nepal, that there is such compression of these religions in a small space in the Kathmandu valley that it is harder there than anywhere else in the subcontinent to sort them out; in fact Buddha and Hindu deities are often worshiped in the same temple — an extraordinary tolerance typical of both religions, unthinkable in the exclusive atmosphere of the Christian denominations.

Not all the temples and shrines felt holy, however, as we discovered on visiting Swayambunath, the temple on the hill which we looked at from our room. *Swayam*, with the same root as the Latin *suum*, means self; *bu* is place and *nath* Lord; the presiding spirit of the ancient stupa is therefore "Lord of the Ground of Self." We expected great impressiveness and made the final climb up through a grove of beautiful old trees with high anticipation and a sense of pilgrimage but in travel, as in other human affairs, expectation is dangerous indeed.

At the entrance to the grove we were accosted by peddlers and "musicians" scraping whining tunes on odd instruments, as well as the usual beggars and children taught to beg, this whole unwanted retinue joined by troops of monkeys. They, too, begged with their sad eyes and anxious faces, holding out wrinkled little hands that were caricatures, in miniature, of the extended hands around them.

From a distance, the stupa, under its gilt top, is a gigantic hemisphere resting on a flat shelf of the hill between its attendant towers, from which a precipitous flight of steps descends toward the valley; but on the platform itself, you are in a hodgepodge of rather ghastly buildings, shrines, miniature stupas and statues, close together as tree trunks in the woods, but all made of stone — like a forest of the most curious stalagmites. Many are barely waist high; some have cubical bases and hemispheres on top; there are long rows of identical seated figures — none of particular artistic merit or interest, all of them smeared and daubed with the vermilion and saffron and black powders which worshipers apply.

In front of one small building which houses the silver statue of a god of healing, several Nepalese were gathered, watching a woman kneeling on the pavement before the shrine. Madhu thought she was in trance, for her body was vibrating all over in an extraordinary manner, her torso swayed like a weed in water and she waved her arms upward and down again in a different, fluttery rhythm, as, also, her fingers. There was no expression whatever on her face. Then, without any warning, she became perfectly normal, rose to her feet and walked away as if nothing unusual had occurred. "She was faking it," Madhu observed, "if it were a real trance she wouldn't come out of it like that, all at once."

At a smaller shrine a monkey suddenly clambered out of a small opening in the wire screening before an image and perched nervously on the sill. When I looked at him closely he went all shy, like a child, and popped back in again, where he resumed shoveling into his mouth with both hands the grains of rice some worshiper had presented to the deity. There were monks about with their shaved heads and yellow robes and many people who acted as if they lived here, yet the entire place was filthy beyond believing, excrement on the pavement, rice grains and discarded flowers and miscellaneous debris whirled into circles in the hilltop wind. Monkeys tore about mischievously, uttering little shrieks, and a procession of dogs streamed in, panting, from the main entrance and broke into a furious fight over a bitch in heat who stood dripping blood onto the pavement. A temple? The place was a kind of madhouse. Why doesn't someone *do* something? I wanted to shout, feeling outraged and depressed, then realized that in a culture where all life is sacred, of course no one would "do" anything: no life process is interfered with, whether this be copulating dogs, thieving monkeys or cows lying down in the middle of the street. It was a kind of vast acceptance which feels to the Western mind like a vast and inexcusable shrug. Yet couldn't they at least clean up a little? Even Madhu seemed depressed by Swayambunath and when, later, we talked with Father Stiller, the scholar-historian, he immediately agreed that this particular stupa had a sadly decadent atmosphere.

Though much of what we saw was strange and foreign, there were representations closer to what we *are* familiar with than many of our own expressions of them: unknown deities attended by the most aerial birds and simian monkeys, the essence of these perceived and portrayed with uncanny insight; bas reliefs and friezes of human figures whose actions and postures made much of our sculpture look artificial and rigid; recumbent Nandi's (Shiva's bull) more alive looking than the live ones lying beside them in the street.

Part of the joy of exploring in Pathān and Badgaon came from discovering treasures of mythological and religious art in the most unlikely places. In a courtyard of a royal palace the king's bath is as encrusted with deities as a medieval reliquary with jewels, the walls covered with exquisitely refined carvings of Hindu gods and goddesses. Diminutive plants and sprays of maidenhair fern sprout from among the carvings, giving a lovely wild tenderness to mysterious and ferocious-looking multiarmed or multiheaded beings. Here, as in most places, worshipers had stuck fresh marigolds and field flowers into crevices of the sculptures and at one niche containing an image of the elephant-headed Ganesha (son of Shiva and his consort Pārvatī) a favorite since he is the god of luck and overcomer of obstacles, a devout old man was tenderly tucking in marigolds and placing individual petals of flowers at various points of the statue, all the while murmuring prayers.

Such decorating seemed charming and touching; less so, the sprinkling of rice and offerings of odd-looking cakes and foods; least of all, the colored powders completely covering some statues and, to our eyes, disfiguring them. But Madhu explained that each color represents an undesirable trait to be gotten rid of — vermilion for aggressiveness, black for lust or greed, and yellow for anger — and that by offering them to a god one rids oneself of them. Maybe it isn't aesthetically pleasing, but what sound psychology!

These evidences of individual acts of worship gave me the same sense of loss I had had on leaving Dakshinkali. Why — given any religious belief — should the carrying out of ceremonies be left only to the priesthood? Why wouldn't people — anyone — not only benefit themselves from such acts but add a positive and beneficent note to the world's feeling-tone? The entire base of the stupa of Budanath is circled, in niches, with prayer wheels: heavily carved cylinders about a foot high and four inches in diameter, which people set revolving as they pass by on their way to shop or field or village well. Before coming to Nepal, I had mentally ridiculed the very idea of prayer wheels but when we were there found it the most natural and gratifying act to set the wheels turning as I moved past them, in each case holding a definite and particular thought toward people I love. Was it silly? Useless? It would seem hard to say — when it isn't even known what thoughts really are.

The good Catholic lights candles and tells his rosary but I was brought up a Protestant and attended services in a simple (and beautiful) white church where, from our pew, the only involvement for the eye was a stained-glass angel with downcast eyes standing in a field of Easter lilies; the only things to do — when my best friend and I weren't trying to make each other giggle or half-choking in the effort not to — were to join in responses spoken in flatter-than-ordinary speech and, of course, to sing hymns. We sang our hearts out; we sang till we grew dizzy from lack of breath: singing helped to offset the endless listening and sitting. Years later, history studies clarified the causes of these austerities, yet if reason was satisfied, I now discovered that another part of my nature was not; that in a subtle way I had even been deprived.

In Hinduism the progress toward enlightenment by means
of individual acts of worship is called prajna-yoga and is
considered the most accessible path for the ordinary man to
follow. The concept of the one, ineffable, formless and
substanceless God — for Hinduism, in spite of appearances, is
a monotheistic religion — is too subtle and difficult for the
common man to grasp; he needs something on which to focus
his attention and devotion. Whether as cause or result, a
whole pantheon of deities sprang up and evolved though it is
more accurate, perhaps, to call it a mythology rather than a
theology. Concrete religious symbols began with the simplest
possible deities — a monkey god, a lion god and so forth.
Since these failed to satisfy human aspirations, new gods were
created, in human form, yet they were subject to death and
therefore mortal; they wouldn't do either. Eventually, therefore, the gods acquired superhuman attributes and powers:
more heads to think with, more arms with which to act and to
hold symbols of power or holiness, such as the quoit or
chakra, the drum, flame, lotus flower.

Little by little as we were exposed to them, the cast of
chief characters in this pantheon became clearer — like the
figures of a fresco in some poorly lit place slowly coming to
life as the eyes grow accustomed to the dark. The great gods
Shiva and Vishnu and their vehicles, Nandi the bull and
Garuda, the half eagle, half man; Brahma and his swans;
Shiva's consort, Pārvatī — sometimes a lovely, sinuous,
womanly creature, at others that terrifying Kālī, brandishing
knives — and Shiva and Pārvatī's potbellied, elephant-headed
son Ganesha with the cheerful expression — all became familiar as the Greek gods had become on my first visiting Greece.
Also, as the confused babel diminished and one was no longer

so preoccupied with who all these strangers were, it was possible to begin seeing the differences in representation and recognize which were finer or more sensitively portrayed.

The effect all these figures have on the mind and psyche, however, is a very different and mysterious phenomenon. I am still teased by the question of what they say to me, and to the Western mind. To those of us who were brought up on the Bible and had any exposure to Christian art, those white-bearded (were they always white?) patriarchs and prophets of the Old Testament, the heroic young boys, Isaac and Joseph, David and Jonathan, the old and faithful women or the young and wickedly seductive were almost as well known to us as those more distant relations whose beings tower so pervasively over one's childhood. The representations of Christ — I can speak only for myself here — were totally other: painful; incomprehensible. How could this man — who wasn't a man but was God himself — be flesh and blood, let himself be excruciatingly killed, reappear, be drawn up into heaven — and do all this to save and forgive *me*? What had I done that needed such savagely extreme sacrifice? Looking at that tortured face and body I felt dreadfully sad, horribly guilty for I couldn't imagine what, or just plain puzzled and embarrassed. (Years later, when I read to a daughter from the same beautifully illustrated book of Bible stories which had been read to me and we reached the story of the Crucifixion, she turned her head sharply to the wall and said quietly and firmly: No, don't read me that; it's too sad and I'm not old enough.)

Beyond the Bible were the figures of those two other worlds — fairytales and myths, the former as natural and part of life as butterflies and toadstools, moonlight and thunder.

Why did grownups put on those faces of sly amusement if they were mentioned when it was so obvious we lived among trolls and nymphs, were visited by sprites and threatened by ogres? The images of myth — and I speak particularly of Greek myths — were the least real of all, perhaps because one came to know them chiefly from that white statuary with blind eyeballs. When I visited Greece they became surprisingly real, even human — on a grand scale — yet now feel more like archetypes of bodily perfection, beauty, prowess. Like Galatea, they all seem creations which become human when embraced, only to return again to pure and marble physiques with expressionless or even vapid faces.

And now in Nepal, there were these extraordinary figures from an unknown world — thronging around, assailing the eye at every turn and having nothing to do with the familial Old Testament, with nature spirits or the ideal human body. What *are* they about?

In front of me, in vivid color photographs taken in the brilliant Himalayan sunlight, are a kneeling, winged man, with a snake around his neck and an indescribably beautiful face, wearing a real necklace of fresh flowers; a king, meditating, in front of a cobra bigger than he is, a bird perched on the cobra's spread hood; a crowned, royal-looking personage holding on one knee a tiny and exquisite woman crowned with more heads than can be counted; most extraordinary of all, an enigmatic-faced woman, probably Kālī, wearing a diadem of skulls and an apron with a ball-fringed border of human heads, like the shrunken heads of cannibals. One of her feet is resting on an alert-faced, fantastic creature — a sort of crested lion-dragon — the other on the body of a kneeling

deer whose head has just been cut off but is still connected to
the neck by tendons and gushing veins. The woman has four
main arms and fourteen subsidiary ones all fanned out around
her, holding among other objects a drum, arrow, sword,
snake, shield, scepter, bowl (of blood?), a flame; the bottom
right hand is prodding with a trident a quite lovely, very
small female figure, whom she holds by the hair with her
bottom left hand.

I can neither comprehend this apparition nor like it, but
neither can I understand or particularly care for some of
what I dream. Those out-of-scale figures and everyday objects importantly illuminated as images of the Grail, the
abnormally vivid organs and intimacies, are disturbing
enough. But what about the beasts and sea creatures which
never were on land or sea, or the iridescent, speaking birds,
the human faces like visions from Paradise or from hell?
Where did *they* all come from? Aren't they just as queer as
the mythological beings of Nepal?

Wandering about in Badgaon and Pathān and Kathmandu
itself, returning to Pathān more than once, I felt as if something at a very deep level was being touched, some vast and
locked region (room is too small a word) was being entered,
or a kind of surgery performed — though whether removing
obstruction, fusing or transfusing I cannot know. Nothing I
have yet seen anywhere is more foreign, more antipodal than
what exists in Nepal yet some part of me responded to it.
Are we, *all* of us on earth, then related? In the most basic
sense, brothers? Do we carry in us, at bottom, the same traces
of everything that has happened to our species — less or more
buried in the unconscious of the individual according to

where on the earth's surface and to what branch of culture our ancestors for the last thousands of years belonged?

It is the question Jung raised, opening wide a whole new world of thought. Once the question is asked, nothing looks quite the same; one is started on a journey to the unknown.

PILGRIMS

THE GUARDIAN SPIRIT, or deity, of Nepal is Pashupathi, Lord of Animals, and Pashupathinath, his temple, the holiest-feeling place we visited. One of the most ancient existing temples, built, it is said, on the site of the oldest known building in Asia, its complex of buildings spreads out on either side of the Bagmati River, which flows, two hundred miles southeast, into the Ganges and is therefore itself a holy river. No non-Hindu may enter the main temple with its gold roof and doors of solid silver; we had to cross over to the opposite bank to see it.

On a high terrace we stood in a long row of recumbent Nandis, behind us another row of small open shrines, each containing the lingam, or phallus, of Shiva. On a pedestal beside us a magnificent trident of gold pronged the sky — symbol of Vishnu and also of the Hindu Trinity of Brahma, Vishnu and Shiva: Creator, Preserver and Destroyer respectively, or — as Madhu liked to put it to help Western minds — the three great principles: Generative, Operative, Destructive.

The river flowed quietly but quite fast between its stone embankments. On the long steps below the temple and on rocks and terraces upstream, people were bathing in the holy water, collecting it in jars to take home or piously sprinkling it on themselves. A poor-looking gaunt man, naked except for a loincloth, squatted on the bottom step carefully cleaning his teeth, as the poor do, with a twig of the medicinal neem tree. Downstream of the bridge we had come over, under a high roof, a body was burning to ashes in a pile of wood while the men of the family sat or squatted nearby, watching.

We recrossed the bridge to leave; beside the steps to the river sat a strange figure in lotus position, eyes closed. His hair stuck out from his head in as many directions as Struwwelpeter's and was matted and thick; his skin was powdered, ashen, even blue — almost as blue as the skin of Krishna in Indian paintings. Like some strange idol, he sat facing a tiny temple to Pārvatī. This was open on four sides, like a garden pavilion, over the *yuni* — a flat, circular form with a channel leading out which is the emblem of the creative female energy of the universe. In front of the closed eyes of the man meditating, a woman touched her forehead reverently to the stone — all sprinkled with fresh flowers — then stepped back and readjusted the folds of her sari. "Mother of the Universe," she said gently to Madhu as she left; she had a beautiful smile. A few feet away, men were loudly splitting logs for the burning ghats, talking as their axes fell and the wood clattered but the blue man never moved.

"What *is* he?" we asked. Madhu smiled. "An American hippie," he said.

One autumn in the late sixties, word went out through the hippie world: "The scene is Kathmandu" and by Christmas hundreds of young people had converged on a city unprepared for such an invasion. Nepal is an open country as regards drugs, a fine (and very strong) grade of marijuana being the one most commonly used, but with the Nepalese people, living far from the pressures of the modern world, drugs have never been a problem. It is a completely agrarian society without a single factory as yet, few paved roads, few automobiles. Except for petty thievery there is no crime and therefore no prison. There are hospitals but no mental cases, no psychiatrists. Inevitably, the foreign embassies, and particularly the American, were besieged with the problems of young people on bad trips, out of funds, in need of help. For several years this was a real headache until, in the case of the American Embassy, a policy was adopted of extraditing to India anyone in that kind of trouble. Some of the young population stayed on, however, and as is often the case, went from drug-taking to meditating and on to studying Eastern mysticism — a very natural step, really, whether as a result of bad trips and the fear of what could happen again, worse; or from the realization that it is possible, and more desirable, to achieve the enlightening experiences of good trips on one's own.

One afternoon I meditated with some of these young people in a small Buddhist monastery on a hilltop six miles outside the town. When the wife of our cultural attaché in Nepal had learned of my interest, and of my having meditated for several years with a group of similarly minded friends, she offered to take me there. Our traveling companions, meanwhile, had flown to Pokhara, in the jungle country, and on to "Tiger Tops" for a few days, leaving us extra time for exploring Kathmandu.

The way — you couldn't call it a road — was so full of potholes and ledges of rock we often preferred to get out and walk, letting the driver manage the plunging and careening

jeep. About a mile from our destination, where Amyas left us
to go off on his own, we came upon others walking our way,
Westerners, mostly, and many young Americans, all climbing
the hill for the regular Sunday afternoon meeting with a
Tibetan lama.

I wondered what he would be like; our group audience a
few days before with the old Cheniya Lama, third in succession,
had been a disillusioning farce. When I'd asked the old boy,
stiff with brocades and gold and probably a harmless enough
showoff, if he knew Chögyan Trungpa (an outstanding
Tibetan whose book I had read) he looked vague, gave the
silver prayer drum in his hand a few merry whirls, then burst
out with, "Nearly everyone knows *me!*" His definition of
karma — admittedly difficult as that concept is — was, in
brief, that if you gave to the poor, built a fine highway and
contributed to the community, then you would be reincar-
nated as a rich man.

The monastery was set in a grove of trees a little below the
top of the steep hill — another child's-drawing peak like that
of Swayambunath — and was a small unpretentious building
which might have been any nice whitewashed house in the
countryside. We were met at the door by Sister Palma, who
was its leading figure — a handsome fortyish-year-old
woman, half American, half Russian nobility, who had had
several marriages and once modeled for a Paris couturier but
now wore rough brown robes and close-cropped hair. At her
side was a little four-year-old daughter born since her marriages; in the hallways were a couple of monks and another
American nun.

We were shown into the meditation hall, where twenty or
thirty people were already sitting in silence on mats and

pillows around and through the room, waiting for the session to begin. I looked at them with interest: a few had haunted eyes and deeply troubled expressions; others were outstandingly strong and beautiful with the kind of face one sees now which I cannot remember seeing anywhere before — serene, natural (without makeup, if a woman) and a look of being about some business other than the rest of the world's or perhaps seeing something the rest of us don't. The faces of men living with the elements and close to nature have somewhat the same look yet are often strained as if from overmuch searching of horizons; these appear content with here and now.

The meditation hall was simple and charming. At the far end, under a painted scroll of the Buddha, a table covered with a white cloth held flowers in small vases and a bowl of sand planted with incense sticks, which Sister Palma came in and lighted. After a period of silent meditation, the Lama walked in and I knew at once it would be all right. Young, probably in his thirties, he had an open, devout-looking face and large, expressive hands; he moved quietly and purposefully, followed by two little dogs (Tibetan, which are like Pekinese), who trotted self-importantly and with happily smug faces at his heels. On the floor in front of the altar, he settled himself, facing us; the dogs flopped down at his feet and went immediately to sleep.

After a few swayings to get his seated position just right, the Lama began to chant and most of the group joined in. Not knowing the chant, I couldn't, but as I sat there surrounded by voices there came one of those magical moments in time when everything seems beautiful and right and feels in perfect order and harmony: a moment of grace and redemption. Outside the windows on either side of the altar, leaves were stirring a little in a gentle breeze, their shadows and the late sunlight drawing delicate patterns on the white walls. The incense and flowers, the curled-up dogs, and the people all united in meditation and chanting were very moving; it was a moment of pure peace and joy.

The Lama then talked to us, in such heavily accented English that I couldn't understand at first more than a word or two here and there. Little by little more words became clear and his sincerity and devotion were such that they helped understanding. What he said about non-attachment and being free of opinion, ridding oneself of the treacherous "this-*or*-that" concepts, was familiar to me — was a doctrine that had originated here, after all, and was imported to the Western hemisphere; this was hearing it on home ground. He went on to speak about "pier" — that was what it sounded like, until I realized that all *f*s came out as *p*s. "Pier," he told us, resulted from and derived its power from misunderstanding. It was caused by something and whatever is caused and arises also comes to an end so that first "pier" arises but just as surely it vanishes. Fear of death, fear of suffering arose from the desire to have it otherwise — whereas acceptance of pain, of the fact of death, relieves fear of it. And fear causes more commotion than the event itself: fear of going to the dentist only adds to the pain of the drill . . . What an odd jolt to hear him talk about dentistry and be transported to my own dentist's, twenty floors above Fifty-seventh Street in New York, with all the latest equipment buzzing and hissing away and piped-in music for distraction. I longed to know more about this young man — where he had come from, what his

experience was. I was sorry we had to leave before the meeting was over.

I also wished later that I could have spoken with the other
American nun, who, as I discovered when I was home again —
and in the best Gilbert and Sullivan tradition — was the long-
lost cousin of one of my close friends. She had, in fact, been
born in my friend's house, in her very bed, but had been lost
track of for years. The nun's own story was anything but a
Gilbert and Sullivan one: an instance of an LSD-induced
psychosis, a turmoil of marriages, liaisons, wanderings, ending
here in Nepal with a six- or seven-year-old son who at one
time was located by our authorities living with Sherpas in a
village far up near Everest. Though I was able to tell my
friend where her cousin was, by the time letters were ex-
changed to verify the address, word came that she had left
and gone to India, the winds of her fate still blowing her
around the world.

It was getting late when on the way down the mountain we
were held up by a cow lying in the track. We had noticed
her when we were going up; she was obviously gravely ill but
lying near enough the edge for the jeep to get by; now she
was right across the track and there was no possible way to
proceed, the land above and below being far too steep. Our
driver got out and tried to coax her, taking hold of her horns
and gently turning her head, pushing against one shoulder
with his foot; when this had no effect, he walked back up to
find help. Two men returned with him and after studying the
situation they all three struggled to move the cow's nearly
dead weight — a pitiful sight — and after many attempts
finally succeeded in turning her body just enough so that with

careful maneuverings, the jeep could pass. She never raised her head or moved a muscle as the wheels passed within inches of her open, suffering eyes. The patience and gentleness of the men's actions, their lowered voices, were touching. I think all of us there were conscious of the nearness of death; the dignity of death illuminated the scene like the lowering sun lighting the mountain grass.

And then, down on the plain again, there was Amyas, striding along toward us across the drying rice paddies — tall, Nordic-looking, smiling: the image of healthy, interested vitality. It was a delicious shock, like a struck bell, seeing him in that foreign place, coming from the direction of the great old stupa of Budanath, which was strung around with prayer flags, the painted, watchful eyes under their black brows looking less protective then menacing. A sense of the precariousness of existence rose like a chill evening breeze. It was good to have him climb into the jeep beside me, hot and rumpled from walking; to be jostled solidly against one another by the impossible bumps of that impossible road.

Now, since these words were first set down I have learned that Sister Palma has died. She had left the monastery where I met her for a year's retreat of intensive meditation near Thubten Cholling Monastery far up in the Himalayas. Her death, the day following a visit from two Peace Corps volunteers, has never been explained. There was, of course, no doctor, no death certificate, no way of knowing what happened to her. And because it was in the monsoon season the news did not get back to Kathmandu for five weeks. The body had been cremated, interment and ceremony held at Thubten Cholling, last outpost of civilization before Everest itself.

RAM LAL

IN ALL ITS STAGES the harvest was fascinating: a gigantic community enterprise, bringing out into the fields everyone but the very aged and infirm. Women did the cutting and laying out of the straw; children helped with easier tasks or played about and babies were laid into little wigwams made of straw in which they slept all day in the shade. The men carried the grain, in fifty- or seventy-five-pound bags or baskets hung at either end of a pole of bamboo across their shoulders, and when the fanned-out straw had dried, they piled this into circular ricks with a central topknot, a shape which looked just like that of the stupas. Standing atop the ricks, wearing loose shirts and the thinnest of straps between their bare buttocks, the men cut fine figures.

The straw to be taken home for fodder or bedding was tied into big bundles, often made into a sort of tepee which completely covered the person carrying it so that all one could see was a seven-foot straw pyramid bobbing along on two feet. The only "machinery" we saw used was treadle-operated threshing drums — hollow cylinders covered with teeth like a larger version of the cylinders inside music boxes. Revolving the drum by stepping on a pedal and holding the stalks against the teeth made the grain fly off; the rhythmical thrump-thrump of the drums' turning gave out a comfortable summery sound, like that which hand-pushed lawn mowers used to make.

From early morning when we first looked out our windows and saw a few people already at work in the sunrise mist until the evening "traffic" of everyone coming home again down dusky lanes and roads, the harvest went on, families and neighbors helping each other out even though each owned his own land. Some of it must be extremely hard work: that weight the men carried on their shoulders, padding along barefoot at a light trot, bodies leaned forward as if to add to the momentum. And the women, cloth wound around their waists or hips in thick twists — to relieve muscular strain, Madhu said — on their feet hour after hour, bending over in the fields with a sickle, or where grain was spread to dry, swinging straw trays in the windless air to winnow it of chaff and dust. Yet they were always gay, their bronzed and ruddy faces smiling; they waved greetings to us and happily obliged when we took their pictures.

They are lovely-looking, the Nepalese women, with a small diamond flashing in one nostril and fascinating ear decorations: a series of little gold rings which follows the outer rim of the ear, swinging and twinkling as they move their heads. Married women paint the middle parting of their hair bright red and wear a special bead necklace with a triple gold ornament at the front center. Both women and girls plait colored strands of wool with a gilded and beaded tip into their black pigtails. Hard-working peasants as they are, they have a very feminine, contented look.

Do I, living in New York in the latter part of the twentieth century and "the latter stages of the rapid decline of Western civilization," romanticize the lives of these people? Admittedly I can have no realistic idea of how it would be to live as they do, but I can observe the expressions on the faces I saw and reflect on what I see on the faces of other hard-working people in my part of the world. Are the lives of those thousands and millions of city dwellers and commuters from the suburbs any easier? Fighting traffic, time pressure, noise and confusion in order to spend eight hours a day tapping typewriters, punching cards, tending machines or doing business on the telephone? The work humans do, like the energy they expend, seems, like water, to seek a level of its own. With few exceptions and as long as they are well and able and interested in living, people drive their activities — or are driven — to a certain pitch, some at backbreaking physical tasks, others at nerve-racking ones. It seems a curious destiny for the highest form of life and consciousness yet achieved on the earth.

We never heard a voice raised in anger all week, only once heard a child cry, when Amyas, Madhu and I were walking in the valley leading to Dakshinkali. Crossing harvested rice paddies and following paths on raised dikes between, we came to a settlement of five or six farmhouses, warm red brick under thatched roofs. A little girl who had come from there passed us on the narrow, trodden trail, a live duck under either arm — a pretty child, poorly dressed but nevertheless with a small diamond in one nostril. She smiled and nodded but must have said something about our coming for when we approached the houses we heard loud crying and Madhu stopped, with a rueful smile: a mischievous older brother was telling a younger one that the foreigners had come to take him away, *away!* We went no closer and stayed only long enough for a quick look. Hens were clucking in the yard, beautiful big cooking pots and water jars, highly polished, hung under balconies; straw and fodder were neatly stacked and dung patties dried on the walls; except for those it could have been a group of Swiss chalets in the mountains. Returning to the main road we came upon the little girl again, standing watch over her ducks splashing noisily about in the muddy water of an irrigation ditch.

Farther up the valley and high above the meandering Bagmati River, we stopped to look at the lowering light on the Himalayas. An eerie sound came from one couldn't tell exactly where or how far away — a hollow tone which I felt I had heard somewhere before and associated, most improbably, with the sea. Someone blowing on a conch-shell . . . could it be? We turned to Madhu, who answered rather seriously: "When a person dies, and they take the body for burning, a man walks out in front, blowing on a shell — how do you pronounce it — a conch?"

As he spoke we saw directly below us a funeral procession of twelve or fifteen people winding along the side of the mountain and down toward the burning ghat on the river. The body was on a litter, covered with flowers and strewn with saffron and vermilion. Before and behind it, the mourners carried what appeared to be small statues, and one man held the same kind of glittery steeple — a "tree" of bright rings of diminishing size — that tops the stupas. The remote and melancholy sound of the conch was repeated at intervals, getting farther and farther away; the procession of figures moving down the zigzag trail vanished from view but the natural dignity and grace of what we had seen brought tears of recognition that this — or something like it — was how the beloved dead might be treated.

Returning toward Kathmandu we were stopped in our tracks: a parachute with a tiny dangling doll-figure swinging from below it was floating down toward the river and was followed by six more — opening like Japanese water flowers in the late afternoon sky. We watched figures land, one after another, in rice paddies, on sandy beaches beside the river, over a ridge and out of sight. A small knot of onlookers stood gathered on a bluff above the river; we joined them and saw that military officials were monitoring the jumps with a lot of special equipment, talking to the plane from which the drops were being made. We must have watched thirty-five or forty jumps, in bunches, ending with three experts who were using Olympic parachutes and one jumper, doubtless the instructor, who landed in the middle of the white cross laid in the sand for a target. Strange, and somehow touching, to share the excitement and interest of the people around us and to find ourselves shouting and applauding with them the final performance. In that peaceful and pastoral setting it felt like a game we had been watching and even though the men huddled around the radio wore uniforms, they didn't look officious or regimented but had the same open and smiling faces as all the Nepalese. It was a nasty jolt to realize what they were, in fact, doing; to be reminded that this peaceful little kingdom lies between two huge powers who, between them, comprise over a quarter of the earth's population.

All through the millennia when conquerors and invasions and migrations were sweeping across the rest of Asia, Nepal — so far as is known — remained whole and undisturbed. It is a tide pool, untroubled by the world's ocean roar; the only destruction it knows that of decay, the passage of time working plants into cracks of sculpture, tipping temples a little off-center. Perhaps this is another reason it is so exhilarating: here is a complete and ancient culture that is still intact — the past alive, with a life that is still whole and good, giving its people a sense of community and fulfillment.

Another afternoon, driving to the far end of the Kathmandu valley to watch the sunset over the Himalayas, we had a personal encounter as unlooked for as the parachutists swarming out of the sky. As usual, Amyas was intent on photographing — finding exactly the right scene and light, the magic moment. We were also struggling to communicate with a driver who spoke no English, and Madhu was not with us: any meeting of importance was simply not in our thoughts.

The drive took us past Badgaon and other, smaller towns; through increasingly hilly farmland carved into steep, swirling terraces of bright gold millet, over a pass and up to a col on which sits the village of Dhulikel. What must be the main road through the village felt rather more like the bed of a brook: with smiles and gestures we left our elderly driver and walked the rest of the way, drawn toward a school playing-field which looked as if it had a view. It had — over the Chinese road winding, a thousand feet or more below, toward Tibet and, over that, across a vast valley divided into successive layers of hills and valleys, the farthest (unhappily) hills of cloud that concealed the peaks.

Almost immediately we were picked up by children, begging. Here, as in India, they were like a plague of flies: soft yet clinging, not to be brushed off; laying a hand on your arm, touching you (very gently) and either looking sad and appealing or else trying quite aggressively to sell a flower they had just picked. But one intelligent-looking little boy didn't demand anything or even look expectant; he seemed interested in us. More extraordinary: he spoke quite understandable English. Where were we from, he wanted to know. America, we said. His eyes sparkled: That was George Washington's country! The eyebrows under a very high, bulging forehead, peaked: New York? Yes. Broad smile. Bi-i-ig buildings, he said, reaching his hands high.

When a silence fell, Amyas and I wondered aloud to each other about a shrub blooming on the slope beyond the edge of the playing field; at once the boy popped down and picked one of the flowers, offering it to me with a charming "thank you." I asked his age. Nine. Name? Ram Lal.

"You speak good English," I told him.

"I have American teacher in school. Bill." He pronounced it, endearingly, Beel.

We were joined by a young girl: his sister, Lakshmi Devi, leaning over sideways under the weight of a hulking two-and-a-half-year-old brother who studied us solemnly. A wise, mature child, she looked; fourteen years old, as Ram Lal told us, for she didn't speak as well as he did. Another boy bigger than Ram Lal horned in on us, the begging kind, trying to sell me one tired and dusty zinnia. We attempted to shoo him away; how did you say "go," we asked our new friend. He told us. What was "man" in Nepali? *Manchi* (it sounded like). "Cow?" for one of these had joined us, too, noisily munching a yard from where we stood, switching a dirty tail. The lesson continued; he was a good teacher.

Leaving the little group we went further up the mountainside hoping for a break in the clouds but returned to find the range still hidden. Let's sit here a few minutes, Amyas suggested, and we waited hopefully, just over the edge of the playing field, among the flowery shrubs. The great sea of valleys at out feet was unutterably still and lonely, a little sinister in the fading light. One truck coming from the direction of Tibet struggled up the grade and around curves far below: we'd hear it, then lose the sound again and pick it up, louder, more grindingly, on a higher note. Sunset, somewhere, lit and relit the clouds with changing shades of rose and gray. Suddenly, from Amyas: "Do you *see* that?" and he pointed. In a window, way up the sky where there should be only air, a pinnacle of sharpest white, harder and whiter than any cloud, disclosed more and more of itself as the cloud cover parted — a ridge, a snowfield, finally an entire cone of vertically corrugated ice. Awed, we watched it for some time. Then we turned our heads and gasped: almost as far east as the view allowed, a triangular peak vastly higher even than the one in the sky-window: Chomolungma itself! Unmistakable, the great South Col, the triangle of Lhotse to the eastward, standing now in a clear sky. In a few minutes the light was gone, the mountains gray, the valleys dead.

We went to find our car, started the drive home. As we rocked and swayed through the village, someone flew out of a house and stood waving: Ram Lal. We waved through the back window of the car till we were out of sight of his thin, eager little figure.

I remained haunted by the lovely intelligence, even more by that delicate, incandescent spirit: a presence that was outgoing yet tactful — that, in Buddha's words, left "no track" — shone in the big eyes set in a head too large for his body.

His cap had looked too tight, his faded burlap shirt too narrow; in the sunset chill when I gratefully pulled on a heavy sweater, he tried to and couldn't pull his shirt closed across his bare chest. Shivering, he had smiled at me: "Cold," he said, without a trace of self-pity. I longed to do something for him, to keep in touch, and before leaving Nepal called the embassy to ask if they knew anything about a teacher named Bill up at Dhulikel. The young man I spoke with said that would be a Peace Corps volunteer; he'd try to find out and call back.

We were taking a last look around our room before departure and two of the floor maids who floated down the corridors in their turquoise saris, looking and chattering like lovebirds, were already waiting outside the door when the telephone rang and I was given the name: Bill Newsom. Back home I wrote him and enclosed a picture of Ram Lal but months went by before his letter came:

"I am the Peace Corps volunteer who lives in Dhulikel, Nepal, and to whom you wrote about Ram Lal, the boy you met while watching the sunset over the Himalayas. I have been on vacation in India and Ceylon . . . Ram Lal and his sister Lakshmi Devi are both good friends of mine and sometimes have tea with me and come to my room to exchange foreign coins for Nepalese ones, but are not my students. Ram Lal is yet too young to go to high school (6th to 10th grade) where I teach, and is in the fifth grade now. He seems to me also to be quite intelligent and to have an outgoing personality and I enjoy his company." (Here followed a page about possible things to send to him and how to ship them.) "About Ram Lal's address, he lives in a small Newari house on the east end of town but they don't use street names or numbers here, so I doubt if a letter would reach him. Also, his family is moving, he says, to another village called Bhawanapati, which is at least a six-hour walk off the Chinese road, beginning ten miles north of here in Panchkal. However, I have been there before, and have a good backpack, and am fond of trekking, so if you send anything for him to me, care of the Peace Corps . . . I will personally see that he gets it, if at all possible . . . Sincerely, Bill Newsom."

More time passed while I collected and found out how to send three books our children had enjoyed — a pictorial geography of the United states, a similar one of the world and an illustrated child's life of George Washington — and a sturdy winter jacket lined with alpaca. Again a long wait during which I was sure the package must be lost, then this word:

". . . [the package] arrived in our office the last week of May and I brought it out to Dhulikel soon after. I met Ram Lal in the street next day (he has not yet moved to Bhawanapati and may not, now) so he came to my apartment and I presented him with the box. After opening it he was so surprised, and pleased, that he really didn't know what to say, he just grinned and seemed to grow about an inch taller with pride in his new coat. He cannot yet read all of the words in the books but had a good time looking at them, with a friend, on the floor of my room, for about an hour. He can read some English, but only a little, maybe the books will give him the impetus to study. In the meantime he will share them with his friends . . ."

Sometimes now, on a late afternoon in New York with the last light going from behind the glittery, lit-up cliffs, traffic snarled and horns blatting like the protests of driven herds, I think of Dhulikel and Ram Lal. And I remember the drive back to Kathmandu in the dusk, so very soon the dark, the road thronged with homeward-bound figures: men carrying bags of rice hung from a pole or all but obscured by piles of straw — walking haymows; some who clapped baskets on top of their straw load and so made grotesque supermen of straw; women carrying babies; men carrying threshing drums; cows and goats, dogs, sheep, donkeys. Never for more than a few hundred feet was the road empty and for most of the twenty miles it was so full we could hardly find a way through, had to nose carefully along, almost brushing people as we passed. The five-o'clock traffic jam! Amyas exclaimed. Through the open windows we could hear, when stopped, the padding of footsteps, the ripple of voices. The air was cool and sweet; the immense sky — clear to the horizon — thick with stars.

HIMALAYAS

FROM SUNSET at Dhulikel until we left Nepal, the Himalayas dominated whatever we did and whatever happened. Very early the last morning we took the Mount Everest flight, forty passengers or so in a turboprop plane. We flew right over our drive of the day before, over Badgaon and the millet terraces, over the pass — flattened to nothing — and at the top, the village of Dhulikel where, nose pressed to the window, I made out the entire playing field. Beyond it came the wild border country and the road winding into Tibet, valleys growing deeper, with fewer and fewer signs of habitation, the summits shifting from rich to sparser green, finally to raw ocher and umber and slaty gray.

Seated on the southeast side of the plane we saw only these "foothills" from our windows, the glittering range on the other side appearing in glimpses beyond the heads of passengers across the aisle. But about fifteen miles from Everest, flying at twenty thousand feet, the pilots turned in toward the range, banked and swung away westward right beside it, putting the mountains on our side. For several breathtaking minutes we were among the huge peaks, so close that their various forms moved past one another in overlapping and continually shifting layers; we peered through between peaks

HOTEL
INTER·CONTINENTAL
TEHRAN

to other peaks, lost that view and picked up another — still holding, if we looked back, Everest: towering another nine thousand feet higher than we were, snow blowing horizontally off the summit in a gale-driven pennant. Needles and pinnacles of ice and rock reared up below from serrated ridges and wrinkled glaciers; walls of rock or corrugated ice rose in a succession of planes to the topmost diamond-sharp skyline. At one moment, passing over a particularly godforsaken foot of a glacier with a muddy moraine creeping across horrid-looking ice, my heart twisted with fear: did the pilots really know what they were doing?

Back in the hotel (how was it possible, only an hour later?), three extraordinary figures stood in the lobby, wearing brilliant orange parkas with large insignia on the sleeves, quilted trousers and outsize boots, their faces heavily bearded and burned: members of the Argentinean expedition to Everest that was still on the mountain and by this time very near the summit.

I went up to the nearest and, as it happened, tallest member of the group — almost a yeti of a man with a huge build and something oddly primitive about him. He didn't understand me; looked troubled and blank at any language I tried and pointed to one of the others. Like his companions, he looked exhausted, eyes hollowed out and burning as if from fever. The one who did speak English said they'd come down for more supplies but that he'd had enough: he'd lost thirty pounds and been snowed in in his tent for four straight days by blizzards with the temperature at forty below. I asked if they'd had any experience with the yeti, as the newspapers reported, and a look as if he'd seen a ghost crossed his face. N-o-o, he answered carefully, they hadn't *seen* it, but they *felt* something . . . At this moment the desk clerk interrupted, new arrivals crowded in and I never heard what it was.

In the evening, after dinner at the ambassador's residence, the guests were shown the film *Americans on Everest*. We saw the same views we had seen in the morning, followed the painful and triumphant progress of the climbers and looked into the same burned-out faces as those of the Argentineans; heard Orson Welles say at the end of the narration: There are no conquerors of Everest, only survivors.

Before this, and with not enough time to return to Dhulikel which we would have liked to do, we had gone up to Swayambunath and found a quiet place away from the turmoil of the temple where we perched on the slope facing the range. We wanted to watch another sunset, felt the need to pay a final homage to the mountains since the next day would be ruffled with the busyness and distractions of departure.

It was quiet and peaceful in the grove, the only interruptions a boy about Ram Lal's age who walked by but without disturbing us, and an inquisitive young monkey to whom I tossed a malted milk tablet, which he turned over and over in his hand, smelled, studied with his head on one side and at last chewed up with noisy relish. From the valley rose the sound of people's voices and the thump and hum of a threshing drum, nothing more. Far below, a line of women cutting rice moved slowly forward in a crescent, just ahead of the lengthening shadow cast by the hill. Lovely, ancient ritual, timeless and healing to watch. Lovely, natural rhythm, growing out of the body's movements, the time it takes to cut growing stalks and gather them together in the hand.

On arriving in Kathmandu (as I have said) I had the sense of time extending out, without limit — of somehow standing in the middle of it. On this last evening the spreading crescent of women harvesting seemed to be acting out that sensation. At home, as all over the Western world, time drives one forward, the feeling is of being propelled (by what?), of hurrying "as though the devil were after you." Here, time didn't come, go, move, speed up, slow down or chase: it WAS. I can't begin to understand this, let alone explain it and I only flounder, trying to tell the next part: I had the strong feeling that the past was still present and, in a dim way, the future too; that there wasn't the slightest need to hurry because one was *inside* time and not on a kind of railroad track, hurtling toward the end.

But then, as certain physicists as well as mystics and time-haunted men have pointed out (Ouspensky and Dunne and more recently J. B. Priestley, to name a few), time is not only the fourth dimension but further dimensions too. Passing time — turning today into tomorrow and tomorrow, grinding mountains down into the sea, releasing the radium out of uranium — is clearly the fourth dimension, as plainly a quality, let us say, of the individual who begins life as an embryo, is born and grows old and decrepit, as is that person's height and width and breadth: time as a further measurement and attribute. But beyond that, it is suggested, are other dimensions of time itself. At "right angles" to passing time — as breadth is to length (to use for convenience a geometrical analogy for something for which we have no analogies) is that state of timelessness we enter in dreams and may sometimes feel when awake — the state of "eternity" mistakenly conceived of as time going on and on indefinitely instead of freedom from progression itself. While as an extension even of *that* — somewhere in the "outer space" of time — there is the heavenly condition of total, creative possibility. Could this be "heaven"? Nirvana?

Many so-called primitive people have utterly different time concepts from ours. The Mayans did, expressed in their extraordinary circular calendar; so did the Zapotec Indians of Mexico, and the inhabitants of the Trobriand Islands in the Pacific still do. In Nepal, I have heard, people living in the mountains measure distances not by space measurements at all but by time: a certain settlement or monastery is as far away as it takes to smoke a number of pipes. Just as we are learning in the West with our increasingly rapid means of transportation that how long it takes to get somewhere is a more realistic measurement of distance than how many miles away it is. What not so long ago seemed a very far-out idea of physics, we have appropriated quite naturally as a function of our thinking, perhaps preparing us for a new, more all-embracing state of consciousness.

And perhaps, as I write this, another dimension of "me" *is* still perched on that distant hillside beside my husband, hearing the faint sounds of voices and threshing drums, watching the women in the grain; the boy passes behind us on his way to supper or wherever it is he is going; the monkey examines that curious gift from afar: a malted milk tablet. And above, in the sky, as ever since they were forced up by the collision of continents, the great snow-houses of the gods turn gold, wild-rose pink, violet — at last going gray as ash. We gather our things together and go home.

Is this memory of it only mine? Or the world's Memory? It seems so unlikely that what goes on inside the brain box happens only in that bony case. By some process miraculous as the storing of experience in the cells of the individual brain, my memory may have become absorbed into a reservoir — vast beyond imagining though no more so than the vastnesses of Space — of countless billions of human memory-moments, adding its infinitesimal spark of light and sense to the consciousness of the world.

India

INDIA

A GREAT LOVER OF INDIA once told me she saw there, right beside the road, a wild peacock standing on a dung hill, shaking out the magnificence of its tail. That is India for you, she said, with an almost Mona Lisa smile. It is a helpful image for the newcomer, wildly swinging as he does between extremes; trying to fit poverty and human misery into the same picture with Arabian Nights palaces and luxuries and the startling splendor of spiritual insights.

One of the last evenings of the trip, as we dined off a beautiful curry, one of our traveling companions leaned across the table and asked what my feelings were about India. Staggered by the question, I replied that it would take me six months at least before I could begin to sort them out. We haven't *seen* India, added Amyas, which — if you consider a week in Kashmir, three different nights in New Delhi and a week's traveling — was true. The interesting thing was that the question, and the replies, set off an explosive string of reactions.

Does any other continent — and of course India is that rather than a country — evoke as violently opposite responses, stir up more visceral emotions? I have found that there are people who want you to hate India and despise you if you don't — a curious and disturbing phenomenon.

The tropical fruit durian is said to have an exquisite flavor once you can get its ghastly stench past your nostrils and, in the same way, it would seem that many Westerners never "get" India to where they can taste it at all. Returning from the island of Elephanta, the woman seated next to me on the launch spoke sadly of this, having herself been born to American missionaries and living most of her life in the Far East. "So many people never can get past the dirt and the smell to perceive anything else," she said. "It's a pity to think what they miss."

The whole subject of excrement assumes prime importance; it simply can't be ignored. For there it is — patties of it slapped up on walls to dry and be used as fuel when, preferably, it should be returned as fertilizer to the fields; filling the air of city or village with its odor; spreading disease and attracting hordes of avid flies; killing off babies; contaminating, reeking, polluting — a mass of foul realities and repulsive associations. As far back as when we were in Afghanistan, watching the children in the animal market collect manure in their bare brown hands and hoard it like treasure, I had been confronted with nursery memories: Nanny in a starched apron clucking like a disgruntled hen as she wiped my bottom; clean, ruffled drawers replacing soiled ones; grownups' wrinkle-nosed and withering expressions like *Pfui* and *Kiki* at my own, or a pet's, "mistakes." Now, in a complete about-turn, I had to accept the presence of excrement, to admit its uses and function as something else than to be flushed away, out of sight and smell. Animal manure is one thing and the warm ammoniac reek of the cowbarn where those quietly chewing creatures deposit their steaming puddings is even comforting. It may be startling to see nomad children hoarding dung yet what else is there to burn in a land of rock, gravel and sand? Human excrement is another matter, the smell of it too intimate, its manifestations of disease too distressing, yet even that becomes part of the whole experience of India — as it is of one's own body, if not of our toilet-clean civilization.

In the midst of this terribly physical reality glows not only the fairy-tale splendor of Moghul palaces and gardens, but the gauzy iridescence of silks and glitter of jewels — every kind of magnificence and color: the wild peacock displays its fullest glory. If these contrasts are hard enough to get into simultaneous focus, there is the all-pervading one between our ordinary sense of what is real and something which feels like as different an order of reality as dreams are from waking. A vivid unreality seems to hover over the surface of things; under the whimsy and childhood fantasies of palaces there are glints of evil; half-remembered nightmares are only a breath removed from broadening and unifying insights. Thus, the traveler coming to India the first time has no sense of sinking into a familiar heritage but mother-naked, as it were, his psyche is exposed to what he has forgotten, never knew or didn't know that he knew.

And on every hand, wherever he happens to be, he is confronted by those amazing, luminous eyes, more than "windows of the soul," disquietingly like soul itself. Being looked at by those eyes is to be given the odd sense of seeing yourself in endless, multiple repetition, in mirror images of every feeling you've ever experienced — and some you haven't and never will. There is no privacy, no hiding from anything at all under that scrutiny of what feels like the whole of mankind.

No, it is too easy to say I love India, or I hate it — and impossibly simplistic to divide it up into its appealing and revolting aspects. Everything seems to be true of India — as it is of the human mind. It is also indivisible, almost anything about it containing within itself its own opposite so that to attempt impressions in words is inevitably to betray what isn't said. Only the Dance of Shiva begins to express it: that inspired vision interpreted in the flame-ringed figure of the god, at one and the same instant juggling the symbols of creation and destruction, continuously dancing the Dance of Life and Death.

BESIDE THE ROAD

IT TAKES ABOUT AS LONG to get clear of industry, traffic and billboards outside New Delhi as outside New York but eventually, after one more clutch of factories, a last small town that is anything but rural, the city ravels out and one is in the country. Elephant grass or acacia shrubs border the road, then very old shade trees, their trunks tremendous, and beyond them the interminable plain with its vast fields, its scattering of people everywhere, at work: ploughing with oxen or harvesting chickpeas; leading water buffaloes to a pond where they wallow up to their eyes in bliss; irrigating with a team of oxen that walk down a ramp away from the well till a skin bag full of water is drawn up and emptied.

Motor vehicles that morning were rare — occasionally a bus or truck, still fewer cars — but the road was alive with living traffic, with people walking and riding bicycles, leading horses, donkeys and cattle. Camels drifted by, their tortoise-like heads held high as if out of water; an elephant lumbered past under enough wood for a bonfire. When monkeys and chipmunks whisked into view and mongooses flowed away into the roadside grass, we began counting the kinds of creatures we saw, like children playing the old game. And the birds! Who would dream one could have fine birding from a bus on Route I? Parrakeets, Alexandrine and pink-collared; peacocks and partridge and quail; sacred ibis and storks; egrets, herons, vultures, "white eagles" and the ubiquitous mynas and doves. Water birds abound because of the many ponds and marshy places and the wide water-filled ditches beside the road. In some of these, choked with water hyacinths and water lilies, people stood waist-deep among the huge pads, collecting the water-lily fruit, which they eat and which looks like a green, knobby Jerusalem artichoke. Edging the water or the road were pink mallow flowers, enormous and unreal as flowers in fairy tales, and evil-looking castor oil plants. Is it just association that makes them appear so sinister? Or the knowledge that a few of the beans, eaten, will kill you?

At midmorning we stopped at a roadside settlement and got out; at once we were accosted by a man with a python wrapped around his neck, another playing a thin and reedy tune to a cobra in a basket and a third twitching at the chain leash on a dancing bear. Cripples dragged themselves toward us in the dust, pointing out their deformities, making uncouth moaning and whining sounds; only the holy man on a bed of nails and the one doing the rope trick were missing. The obvious fakery was as distressing as the cripples, yet they and the snake charmer knew what they were doing while that mangy bear, dust flying from his fur — what indignities were being imposed on him that he couldn't understand. Though it bothered me, I kept looking at him, the way one unintentionally but persistently keeps biting at a sore place in the mouth: that hairy chest and belly were so like a caricature of a man's, the front paws waved so aimlessly and the silly, small snout tilted skyward because of the way he was being

held. He must have come from far away — maybe the forested hillsides of Nepal. Wondering, I had a sudden vision of
the water-soaked *alpage* of our Swiss picnic, an almost bodily
shock at how far away that seemed — in miles, in time and in
that sovereign of distances: the difference in consciousness.
Switzerland, from here, felt as familiar as New England, and
both equally remote.

The second day, farther from Delhi, we passed or drove
through village after village — a tiny fraction of the half
million villages of India. At the early hour when we started
out, the light had that magic it still has in certain parts of the
world, the light that must have shone over Eden on the first
day. Women gathered at wells with their water jars were
washed with gold or outlined with light as they let the jars
down on a rope to be filled, then walked away home bearing
them on their heads: the earthen jar topped with a shiny brass
one and on top of that the rope coiled into a crown. With
their saris in rich shades of saffron, rose, violet, apricot —
their queenly carriage, they were beautiful archaic figures. In
village streets, light irradiated the fragrant smoke drifting
from food stalls where people were eating their first meal of
the day, and small groups squatted around a steaming pot
from which the shopkeeper ladled out servings. Outside of
houses, right beside the road, old men reclined on their rope
beds in the sun, looking paradoxically like Romans at a feast,
watching us as we passed.

Between villages, as far as one could see — and with no
underbrush or weeds to break the distance — people and
animals dotted the entire landscape. No such thing as an
empty field: the earth grew people and creatures as it did
crops and trees. That man plowing, the other one raking and

leveling with a flattened log dragged by oxen, the boys herding goats and the group of men out in the middle of a field, gathered around a samovar of tea — were as much part of the land as the brooding trees, the green waves of grain. These particular people will vanish, to be replaced by others in an endless, timeless succession — the still center of time's turning wheel. They make the soil of India rich; they sanctify its air. And now, facing them as they go home — painted on a conspicuous wall of every village — is the Family Planning sign of man and wife with two children between them, and, we were told, it is beginning to have its effect.

The only other modern sight was the road itself, crowded now with cows — horns painted bright colors and some wearing wreaths of flowers or decorative crowns. Twice we passed a pullulating heap of vultures on a cow, dead beside the road — exactly like vultures on a kill in Africa. Jostling and cackling and wing-beating their way over each other to the dead center, they covered the carcass so completely not even its color could be seen. Out of the convulsive activity at the center of one of these heaps rose a dog whose face was a mask of blood; somehow avoiding the rapacious beaks and whipping wings, he swam out of the heaving whirlpool to the safety of the grass where he stood, blind with blood, tongue reaching up for and catching it — a nightmare figure far more frightful than the carrion birds.

At the border between the states of Uttar Pradesh and Rajasthan, we stopped in the middle of a village to fill out documents. As in all of the villages, the houses seemed to grow out of the earth, were like the earth molded upward into walls, many decorated with geometric designs scratched into the mud or applied in ridges, like the scars and weltings

on the bodies of certain primitive tribes. Manure patties dried
on the walls or were neatly stacked in piles; the ground was
rutted and filthy. People began coming around the bus out of
curiosity, not begging or seeming to expect anything, just
looking at us and watching what we did, as we did with them.
Women held up babies and smiled; runny-nosed children
craned their necks and stood tall to see inside the bus better;
we were addressed by pairs and pairs of luminous, friendly,
gentle eyes.

This village was one of the poorer ones, its odor powerful.
Behind me in the bus a voice protested: "It revolts me."
What did? I asked. The village. I wondered, and still do, *if*
there is no drought or famine — admittedly a huge *if* —
whether life in such a village is anywhere near as bad as in
Harlem or the South Bronx. Certainly the babies looked
healthy and well-fed and everyone in the little crowd around
us seemed happy. Here in India as in Nepal we almost never
heard a child cry, and the most frequent response to the many
photographs my husband took of people along the way is:
"How *happy* their faces are!"

I believe it is this which the foreigner finds more intolerable
in the East than the smell of excrement: how dare people
living in mud houses and filth look so happy, generally hap-
pier than his own countrymen do? An entire system and
culture is challenged; worse still, the myth on which most of
the activities of nearly two hundred years have been based is
suddenly shown up as perhaps one of the deadest dead ends of
history. What an investment to have depreciated! No wonder there are people who want you to hate India.

As the hours and villages passed, all those faces and figures,
so fleetingly glimpsed and representing every stage and varia-

tion of human life, gradually flowed together into a stream. Without the trappings of crowds in Western cities or the complexities of civilization's buildings and inventions, there was nothing to distract from the sheer stream of humanity, thick with the sorrowful human condition, magnificent with dreams, deep with dignity. The thousands of faces merged into *the* human face, the light of consciousness in its eyes bright with reflection, dark with the awareness of dying. Before that face, the patterns of my own existence, my usual preoccupations appeared faraway and vastly strange; just thinking about them started uncomfortable misgivings rather like the first intimations of having eaten too heavy food. I remembered how Svetlana Alliluyeva (Stalin's daughter) wished to settle for the rest of her life in a particular village of India and could now understand it, but that wasn't the issue. What nagged and weighed was the recognition that the precarious complexity and artificiality of affluent, technological society all but remove me from reality: I live at a distance from almost everything — communicating and communicated with, much of the time, by wire; provided with food from unknown places and across unknown distances; seeing life in pictures or behind the glass of a moving car; breathing air that, if it isn't poisoned, is a mechanically distributed draft. In retrospect I see that, in Jung's words, it is quite possible that India is the real world and that the white man lives in a madhouse of abstractions . . . that life in India has not yet withdrawn into the capsule of the head, it is still the whole body that lives.

And the working relationship of that body is with other bodies like itself or with animals: everywhere, people with creatures instead of people with machines are timing themselves to the trot of a donkey or lope of a camel, the huddled pattering of herded sheep. The curious grandeur of India, hard to define, is immediately apparent outside of cities in this creaturely pace and rhythm of living. The measured movements of oxen ploughing, like the deliberate moves of cattle in the streets — so exasperating to the hurrying Westerner — the stately walk of the women, are ancient, slow, in tune with the earth and its seasons, the procession of sun and moon, night and day.

As the hours passed on this second day's drive I kept wondering just how we would ever emerge from the twentieth-century insulation of our bus and become part of the scene. If there was one thing we had thoroughly learned in the countries we'd been in, it was that you are never alone for long, even in the loneliest-looking places: you make a stop — no one in sight — in a grove by a river, an empty field, and within a minute someone (or a group of someones) is there, looking at you as though you had just stepped from a flying saucer. Here, in country already alive with people, we would certainly collect a crowd, while finding a place to picnic that wouldn't disturb a farmer's crop and would be even moderately clean seemed quite a problem. The solution was totally unexpected.

In the middle of a bustly small town named Mowaha, our guide, Raj, had the driver take us to an inn for a few minutes' stop, but when we saw how charming and private the walled garden was, it was decided that we would stay. The owners of the inn were immediately, smilingly helpful even when Raj made clear to them that we had brought our own food. Long deal tables were carried outdoors and chairs set around; lunch boxes were opened as parrakeets screamed in the trees overhead and bee-eaters flashed about us like flying jewels. Of course people appeared at once, climbed and looked over the high wall, materialized from garden corners — though none was importunate or begging. Enjoying a delicious meal of hard-boiled eggs and roast chicken, cheese and cold beer, I felt guilty about the endearing inn people till we saw we had more than we needed and began sharing it with them where they stood deferentially in the background. Their gratitude was beautiful and touching; the food seemed suddenly to be blessed.

Then a strange thing happened. Amyas, holding up an English "marie biscuit," remarked to John that it was "a typical English biscuit." "Must be if you call it that and not a cracker," John and I answered with amusement and almost in the same breath. At that instant, a curious commotion: a swoop and swift draft; a winged shape retreating before us that we saw with astonishment was a hawk. It had dived between us, leaving on Amyas' finger a small bright wound from its talons. Someone fetched ointment and a Band-aid and as we stood around and marveled I thought how curious it was that I had written a poem many years before about another true episode of a hawk diving on a boy and wounding his hand. What did it mean — this hawk falling out of high noon in India? A peregrine it was, now virtually extinct in the United States due to poisonous insecticides. Read into it what you wish or read nothing at all but a bizarre occurrence; to me it is a message from the world of the wild we are determined to annihilate. We will be lucky indeed if nothing important is taken from us and we are not gravely hurt.

THE PEACOCK

FROM THE TABLE-FLAT PLAIN, simmering to the horizon in waves of heat, the traveler going westward from Agra climbs a long gradual slope. On one side are outcroppings of pinkish red rock, on the other increasingly distant views; the air grows steadily cooler with the climb. At the top of the ascent the hill levels out just enough to carry on its summit the abandoned "Fort" of Fatehpur Sikri, palatial residence built by Akbar the Great in gratitude to a saintly hermit on the hill who — through a miracle — gave the Shah and his wife the son they had longed for for years. The son was Shah Jehan, builder of the Taj Mahal. At the saint's death it is told that Akbar and his entire entourage moved away, having built for the saint the most beautiful tomb that could be devised, in which sunlight and moonlight penetrate to his bed through screens of marble lace and the dome over his head is luminous as pearl. Another, more likely explanation for the abandonment of all that grandeur is that the water supply failed; the artificial lake at the foot of the hill dried up.

Like other palaces in that hot climate, the Fort encloses a succession of open, grassy courts, secret gardens and pools with reflecting or shivering surfaces, but the strange red sandstone buildings around them are of unusually fanciful design, as if highly imaginative children had been able and allowed to build the finest play-city they could dream up. It has not only a greater number of individual "palaces" — pavilions, really — for members of the family, but arches, porches, colonnades are piled one on top of another and little pillared cupolas sit on top of the whole. One large outdoor court is laid out as a Parcheesi board on which the game (which originated here) was played with ladies of the court for counters; a large roofed-over space, crammed with pillars, was designed by the emperor for playing blindman's buff with his harem. Downhill and a short distance away from the palace, a single tower thrusts up through the canopy of trees as a monument to the Shah's favorite personal elephant — but in the outdoor audience court, large as a town square, there is evidence of a more sinister use of those marvelous creatures. To the massive stone ring standing upright in the ground, a mad elephant was tethered, and convicted criminals were thrown under him as the crowd watched. The crime rate during Fatehpur Sikri's occupancy is said to have been extremely low.

Elephants are important in India for more than the work that they do. They are supposed to have supported the four corners of the universe on their backs and the elephant is the "vehicle" of the god Indra; Ganesha, son of Shiva and the god of luck, has an elephant's head. In exquisite miniature paintings of battle scenes, you see the Maharaja of Udaipur's horse wearing, like a mask, an elephant's trunk so that he might be singled out in the fray. (Why not antlers, or a unicorn's horn? They would look better on a horse.) The ancient majesty of elephants, the rhythm of their motions which seems to belong to earth rather than its creatures, are like

India itself. Yet that same Moghul, and probably others as well, used to sit on a viewing balcony at the top of the palace and safely watch inebriated elephants fight one another in the entrance court a hundred feet below.

Do palaces express their occupants? Or are they encrusted with the tastes and ambitions of their architects, even the unfulfillable dreams of the populace? Coming from a part of the world whose royal residences are impressively formal and symmetrical, it is astonishing to visit the Royal Palace of Udaipur — a quarter-mile-long accretion of courts, cupolas, balconies, arcades and porticos, all interconnected by a net-work of narrow passageways, steep little stairways and five-foot-high doors. Dominating the lake and the town like a cliff of white sugar frosting, it is even more of a child's dream palace than Fatehpur Sikri, having a playful, irresponsible, festive quality and a number of entertaining things for its occupants to do without having to leave its airy recesses for the squalid and crowded streets below.

At the very top, for instance, five or six stories above the entrance court, there is a large bathing pool set in the shade of twenty-foot trees, the palace having been most ingeniously built around the top of a hill. In the surrounding colonnade as in several other courts, swings were hung from the ceiling beams, the heavy rings still firmly in place. What could be a more delicious way to cool off! In another open room, in two adjoining tanks each cut out of a single block of marble, courtiers and court ladies used to bathe — at certain festivals in water which was colored and which they threw at one another — and from many places around the building you can step out onto a delicate balcony projecting like a theater box, its roof topped with a finial of crystal, and look out over the city on one side, the lake of Udaipur on the other. Entertainments were held in special courtyards, their walls glittering with trees and vines made of inlay of convex, colored mirror — one with panels of peacocks, every feather, down to the least filaments of the tail, a flashing and sparkling poem. Even a bit of psychedelic fancy was introduced in certain windows whose squares of red, blue, green and yellow glass gave the illusion of seeing the same landscape in winter sunrise and by moonlight, in monsoon and midsummer sunlight — that violent blaze to which the powerful and wealthy never needed to expose themselves.

Twice we stayed in palaces: former residences of Maharajahs converted to hotels. Vast structures, both, with the odor of dilapidated splendor, staffed by servants who, as if under a spell, appeared to have lost their understanding or the powers of locomotion, or who huddled in corners, fast asleep.

One of these hotels was the Lake Palace, an island out in the Lake of Udaipur within sight of the Royal Palace. Here, like everywhere else in the world today, a tug-of-war between the past and the future was taking place. In order to care for more guests, one of the palace wings was being totally reconstructed — size of the garden cut down and stories added so as to fit in as many modern, motel-type rooms as possible, the management seemingly unaware that this updating would subtract from the essence of what was there and ensure the staff a future of bitter scenes over accommodations.

Meanwhile the construction area that guests had to pass through to get to the public rooms — finding their way through tunnels, over boards laid in mud — might have been a scene in Egypt in the reign of Cheops. Scaffoldings of wooden spiles, lashed together with rope, latticed the façade; basins of cement were handed from man to man up a human ladder of six people until, at the top, a figure in a sari, like a colorful bird poised in the sky, gracefully tossed the empty basins down to a man waiting below. The whole operation proceeded in a surprisingly energetic rhythm, accompanied by loud and cheerful singing. It began at daybreak and except for a recess at midday continued until dark — an outrageous imposition on hotel guests yet with an archaic naturalness to it that was delightfully satisfying.

Other ancient traditions were being carefully kept alive, such as the native folk dancing performed certain evenings each week. Chairs were set out in the grass of an open court-yard, one end of which made a natural stage of extraordinary beauty, its proscenium arch a bower of red Indian honey-suckle, the top of the stage a sculptured marble frieze — white embroidery against a sky in which hung a few great glittering stars.

Two dances were outstanding, one a classic *kathak* (thought to have originated before the time of Buddha) performed by a marvelous-looking man in golden yellow tunic and orange silk trousers, silver earrings swinging in his ears and three hundred bells on his ankles. These he rang as he wished, fast or slow, stamping to add a percussive effect, working up to terrific, high-speed twirling in which he became fixed into a loudly jingling top of spinning colors; or by slowly and seductively dragging a big toe across the floor, he shuddered the bells — as a harpist will quiver but not pluck the strings; as the monk at Budanath, in Nepal, had shuddered his cymbals. It was a highly sophisticated, sensual perfor-mance, by a dancer who was both virile and delicately subtle

— at once more masculine and more feminine than we are accustomed to in either sex, as if the qualities heightened for being in combination.

The other dance — an allegory of the young village wife, anxious to please a husband who piled more and more bowls on her head to carry — was danced and mimed by a lovely sixteen-year-old in glittery red, with a jeweled crescent moon in one nostril and bells on her ankles. A ravishing smile greeted each new burden; under the load her body moved sensuously and sinuously, her feet with their bells flickered at high speed, her hands — the fingers like separate characters — acted out vividly the drama of each successive episode. At the end she was dancing with five superimposed bowls on her sleek head.

On the town's lakeside steps, we watched from a boat the next afternoon women balancing jars and bowls on their heads come down to the water's edge where other women rinsed out saris the colors of zinnias, or swayed as they sat washing their bare, brown bodies. The whole scene, gilded by late sunlight, was waveringly duplicated in the water — a dream of itself, as the women were of the folk dance, or the dance was, of them — as everything we were seeing seemed a dream of something else.

*

Very slowly the displaying peacock revolves and poses. Uttering the hysterical shriek of a madwoman, and with a sound like that of a bare branch in a gust of wind, it shakes out the magnificence of its tail and holds it spread, but however beautiful, even hypnotic, the effect, there is also something vaguely ridiculous about the sight: it is hard to take the bird himself too seriously. The peacock, in India, is the vehicle of the war god, Skanda-Karttikeya — a fine example of the brilliant insight of myth. In spite of outdoor Parcheesi courts and enchanted vistas framed in scalloped doorways, the preoccupations of the powerful and proud, here as elsewhere, are war, the art gallery a vivid celebration of battle scenes, such as one in which an invading Mongol with scimitar upraised to bring down on the Maharajah has been perfectly bisected from scalp to groin and the two halves, spurting blood, are just beginning to fall apart. When you want to impress, show what a good fighter you are; we still greet visiting potentates with gun salutes, massed military, screaming jets.

All the more marvelous that the most beautiful building in India, if not the world, built by a great and powerful (and warring) man, is a monument neither to war nor to God but to human love — and like human love it has the power to transform.

*

A certain wealthy and distinguished grandnephew of Ralph Waldo Emerson's, who lived for many years in the Far East, brought back to Boston with him a model of the Taj Mahal in marble and alabaster and inlay, which he placed in a room entirely by itself. After dinner, his guests were taken to this room, the door closed, and they were left for a couple of minutes in total darkness until, very slowly, the Taj became revealed — by artificial moonlight, at dawn, finally at midday. On several occasions I was among the guests and enjoyed each time an effect which was beautiful, the tricks involved in producing it being most cleverly done. After this

I felt I knew what the Taj looked like — much more than from just photographs and slides and postcards. Great heavens, we *all* know what the Taj looks like, as well as the house across the street! Going to see the real thing, I was in a neutral, even skeptical mood (but trying to keep an open mind, so I thought). Then I discovered, as thousands are doing all the time, that I was totally, absurdly, wrong: it is quite impossible to imagine what the Taj is like.

What makes for the surprise? Partly, its sheer, unexpected size — the dimensions are so vast that the building and its approaches easily absorb masses of people (and are enhanced by them); the entrance level, which appears to be about one story above the pools, is actually approached by three flights of stairs. Another feature, just as unphotographable, is the sense of space, height and exhilaration given by the positioning of the building on its wide terrace far above the river. Who would ever guess from pictures the feeling that this gives of being on an acropolis, in the sky? Or have any clue to the way the composition of the whole changes as you walk up to it? Hardly staying the same from any two points, it seems less a building than a living shape which, like a partner in a dance, moves with you as you move.

Guides will tell you that the four minarets at the four corners lean out at six degrees from the vertical so that if there were a catastrophic earthquake they wouldn't fall against the building. I doubt that this is the reason; that slight but perceptible slant gives room to the central mass and pleases the eye, just as does the upward bowing of the Parthenon from both ends toward the middle which makes it float on its height of bare rock. As I remember the story, the designers of the Parthenon had a terrible fight with Pericles over this feature; one wonders if Shah Jehan's architects had the same.

Pictures of the Taj do give a hint — though only that — of its transcendent serenity. Contemplate this long enough and it discloses itself further as a sublime-feeling fusion of opposites, for the Taj is both erotic and chaste; massive and delicate; cold and spare as bone, yet, with all the leaves and vines and flowers of inlay and bas-reliefs, as fluid and full of movement as life. But the greatest surprise of all was, to me, its overt eroticism. Monument to love, and to a deeply loved woman, it memorializes in the most symbolic way the female body — the central arch pure vulva, the dome above suggestive of the womb. The minarets, of such a different kind of construction — blocks of white marble set in courses, like bricks, with sharp black between — typify virility and strength even without their phallic suggestion. The whole, especially at night when there is a flush of warm light at the base of the central arch, is a celebration of warm and open femininity, supported and sustained by the male. Long after we had come home I found that Jung had written of the Taj that it was "Eros in its purest form." He called it the secret of Islam, thoroughly un-Indian but "like a plant that could flower in the rich Indian earth as it could nowhere else."

Sometime in the late afternoon — I have no idea how long after we had first entered the grounds — we sat down on the grass, in silence, and watched — not just looked — as if the Taj were something alive, which it very nearly is. Marble and cloud, its roundnesses varied slowly with the lowering light; whiteness grew iridescent as pearl, then honey-gold; went, quite abruptly, pale and dead. Though figures in saris still bordered the long pools, their reflections glowing in the water

like beds of flowers, the crowd began to drift through the
entrance arch and leave.

At night we returned. The moon was within a few days of
being full, yet surprisingly, almost no people were about and
those who were, were quiet, reflective and worshipful. From
here and there came singing: a plaintive-sounding chant from
a group sitting quietly on a bench; a single voice and responses from one of the mosques adjoining the Taj itself. We
entered the tomb chamber: the light on the walls, coming
from the single hanging lamp of pierced brass, was scattered
with shadows as if from foliage; the voices of three men talking in low tones resonated like a swarm of bees. They left
and we were briefly alone with the old cripple who guards
the tombs; the silence was complete. Then two young men
entered, one with a wooden flute, and he played a phrase. It
had an unbelievable effect: the whole chamber responded
with such perfect resonance that it seemed simply a continua-
tion of the phrase, not an echo. He tried a trill next; impossible to tell when he stopped and the walls took it up. We
spoke to one another and out on the steps sat down and talked
more; he was on the way to Nepal with a group of students
and was eager to hear our impressions.

It was very hard to drag ourselves away — instinctively
walking backward as if from royalty, so as to miss nothing —
so beautiful was the total atmosphere of the soft night, the
gentle sounds of water and of singing, the floating, perfect
statement of the building, glittering a little here and there
under the stars as light from the moon found and glanced off
particular bits of semiprecious stones. Little by little as our
distance from it grew, it became less compelling, more unreal,
then a bubble — and finally the wraith of a bubble.

A horse and carriage took us back to our hotel, the hoof-beats loud in the country quiet, the fields on either side of the road white with mist. We went up to our room and into the night as if just discovering one another — as if we had been separated for a very long time.

SHIVA

By NINE O'CLOCK, when the launch leaves the dock in Bombay for the island of Elephanta with its cave temples, the air was already oppressively hot and still, the surface of the harbor glazed with sun. It was a relief to have the boat push away out of the slosh of waves against the embankment and move a breeze into being, to sit in the shade of a canvas awning stretched over our heads. We were about thirty passengers; mostly Indians and other Asiatics, another American couple, who had lived most of their lives in the East, and the young flight crew of a Lebanese airliner — full of vital good spirits and not at all disturbed by the heat of the sun which lay on us like a weight but which they basked in up on the forward deck. As we puttered past innumerable anchored freighters, tankers like floating laboratories, long docks and breakwaters and even a few sailing vessels, their canvas slatting, the air off the water was dank rather than salty, the enormous harbor stretched interminably away into haze.

An hour out and a short distance from the green hill of the island, the launch slowed to a stop and rocked in its own waves as the engines were turned off and we were addressed by our guide. A rather soft and dull-looking man I had

thought when I first saw him; I didn't listen too carefully to
his facts and figures about Bombay harbor — though I was
surprised at the mention of nuclear reactors and atomic
energy plants — but then he gave us a skillful sketch of the
island and in the most sensitive way prepared us for exactly
what to expect in the timing and effort involved in visiting the
caves as in all the details of the tour.

On our way up the two hundred and twelve steps from the
pier — walking slowly in the breathless heat — we were
passed by one of our companions, a stout and heavily sweat-
ing Indian woman, being briskly carried up in a chair by four
bearers. At the top there was a fine view out over treetops
and water to hills on the opposite shore. As the group waited
there for all to assemble, monkeys began coming out from the
woods, glancing about with questioning faces, and someone
threw a banana, then another, and more fruit followed. The
animals stuffed themselves till their throats bulged like goiters
and one baby monkey made off with a whole banana which
provoked a lot of laughter and joking. My heart sank: was
this another Swayambunath? I remembered the words of a
friend who had visited the caves thirty years before and who
urged us to go. "But I have no idea what has been done to
them by now," she added. "For all I know they may be lit up
with neon lights and have Coca-Cola concessions at the entrance."

Our guide waited for the end of a story someone was
telling before gently gathering our attention. The caves were
now only a short distance away, he said, and were very
holy — one of the holiest places in India; he would tell us all
he could about them but it would be best if we would save

our questions till later and keep as quiet as possible. As he spoke his face became lit with a kind of grave joy, the prominent eyes brimmed with feeling.

Like children following a teacher, we straggled behind him along the paved walk that circles the hill, in and out of the shade of forest trees and across a terrace, the monkeys accompanying us eagerly part of the way. Then they fell behind, we turned away from the water and entered the hill.

*

The cave temples of Elephanta are dedicated to Shiva — one of the Hindu trinity which includes Brahma, the Creator and Vishnu, Preserver. But Shiva is also thought of as the Supreme Deity encompassing and merging their aspects in himself — Shiva as the "Great Lord." We had seen his gold trident at Pashupatinath in Nepal and a great number of representations of his vehicle Nandi, the bull; also his lingam, the phallic shape symbolic of the generative energy of the Universe; all of them interesting objects and some of the Nandis beautiful yet still only emblems — the traces and evidence of a presence but not the presence itself. That had first struck me in a magnificent bronze sculpture, *The Cosmic Dance of Shiva*, exhibited back at Asia House in New York. The poised figure with whirling arms and mysteriously impassive face, balanced in a ring of flames — the sense it gives of the furious yet harmonious interplay of forces — symbolizes with the compression of poetry and myth and dream language the nature of the universe. The hands of the figure, one holding the drum that summons creation, another the flame that annihilates, represent and embody the continuous creation and destruction of matter which is an essential feature of the cosmos. Ancient it may be, it is also as contemporary as nuclear physics.

"Shiva is the manifestation of the primal rhythmic energy that keeps the cosmos alive." Those are the words not of a philosopher but of a nuclear physicist. And just how the matter of the universe *is* alive, "creating and destroying particles at a dazzling rate," physics now explains, and proves, in the quantum field theory. Modern science and the intuitions of ancient mythology are in perfect accord on this basic interpretation of Life.

The beauty of that sculpture and the comprehensiveness of its symbolism drew me back again and again. It seemed to express everything possible to express about the indivisible and living nature of the universe; it kept coming to mind in a growing number of connections. I hadn't thought anything was missing — or, rather, that I missed anything in it — until Elephanta.

Cave is something of a misnomer, as is temple; the reality is neither, and both. A rocky cliff near the top of the hill may have had a deeply indented ledge with an overhang, like some of the caves in southern France, but whatever was there to begin with, unknown stonecutters and sculptors carved a central chamber and two smaller side chambers out of the solid rock, leaving supporting pillars at regular intervals and covering the inner walls with bas-reliefs, also chipped out of the "living" stone. The central chamber goes one hundred and thirty feet into the hill and is the same measurement wide; the rough ceiling is twenty feet overhead. To the great credit of the Indians there isn't a single light bulb and the nearest bottle of orange squash is back through the woods at the top of the steps up from the pier. They don't even like having

many people in it at once — at least our guide didn't: when
another group came in while we were there, he said he would
stop talking until they went farther away so we wandered
about on our own until the chamber grew quiet once more.
He was a jealous guardian of the mysteries he so clearly
worshiped.

These begin right at the entrance where two great bas-
reliefs face each other in the dramatic opposition of Shiva
dancing and Shiva meditating — the first where he is "Lord
of Dancers," a study of the stillness at the heart of motion, the
other, "Lord of Yogis," of the movement in apparent stillness.
"At the still point there the dance is . . ." The figures are
mutilated, some of the arms and legs have been shot away by
invaders' cannons and vandal fanatics, yet the two aspects of
the same beautiful and calm absorption are as compelling as
the two poles of a magnet.

It is the same with the bas-reliefs that surround the inner
chamber, where other, different aspects of Shiva are shown in
opposition: where, across from the Destroyer in the full fury
of destroying, he stands as tender and loving bridegroom
beside the most enchanting Pārvatī. Creation keeps alternating with destruction, violence of purpose with gentleness of
acceptance; there is continual variation within the same being — a being that says: I am this — and I am also *this*, its
opposite. The allegory of dualities of being culminates in a
marvelous androgynous figure of Shiva, of which the right
side is male and the left female, not only in physical features
but in expression and feeling. Each pair of bas-reliefs rein-
forces the statement as does the magnificence and grandeur of
the figures.

These are considered as fine as any sculptures in India and
to many people (I am one of them) the finest they have seen
anywhere. It is hard to believe that such minutely subtle
variations of facial expression can be achieved at all in mountain rock of massive proportions or that the flying gods and
goddesses and angels — all the heavenly hosts floating above
and around the main figures — can be so ethereal and alive.
When one realizes that there was no margin whatever for
error and once the rock was chipped off it was gone, the
sculptures become a miracle of execution as well as of spiritual
insight.

We moved farther in, and away from the brilliance of the
outside world. The light, coming partly from below and off
water, made the interior gently luminous; the air smelled
stony and cool as we walked past rows of massive pillars that
are still part of the hill. I saw that halfway up, their squared-
off shafts become circular and fluted like ridged stems — very
fat at the bottom and tapering inward as they rise till, just
under the roof, they bulge out into rounded caps or cushions.
They are tremendous mushrooms of stone.

Our group, silent and attentive, was now drawn toward the
central image against the inner wall facing the entrance, and
known as the Mahesamurti: the twenty-foot-tall triple head
of the "Supreme Shiva, fully manifest." To the left, seen in
profile and in deep shadow, is the face of violent aggression
and destruction, with a serpent held in one raised hand; to the
right and also in profile, the powerfully creative and protective face of the feminine principle, the hand holding a lotus.
Centered between them, eyes closed, is the sublime transcen-
dence of these and of all opposites which tear the individual

being apart or combine in creative tension — a head which is
the image of elate calm, of majesty, and of containment
totally free of time and space.

I looked and saw what I didn't know existed: divinity made
visible — and in human guise. I was stunned and struck with
recognition — both: here was something which had always
been missing yet I hadn't known that it was. Faces transfigured by emotion may hint at it but are only approxima-
tions; those in paintings and sculptures of saints and angels
and heroes; of Christ and his apostles — of whatever period
or region — feel like sketches for it but however perfect in
themselves, however great as art, they have not yet arrived at
this ultimate spiritual grandeur.

What are the closed eyes contemplating? What being
is so at peace with the turmoil, horror and delights of the
world? Though human, the face is that of the *Bhagavad-
Gītā*'s "This (which) never is born and never dies, nor may
it after being come again to be not; this unborn, everlasting,
abiding Ancient . . . not slain when the body is slain."

Once in my life I had felt an intuition of this Being, and of
the saying, "*That* art thou," when, coming out of anesthesia
and still under drugs, I seemed to know quite clearly that my
own nature was without age or place — that it had always
been and so would always be, that this nature was my true
self though in no way "mine" . . . But were I to say that on
looking at the Mahesamurti I was enlightened or had what the
Buddhists call satori, it wouldn't be the truth. It was one of
those moments when the surface of life cracks open and the
sense of time is shaken like disturbed water though months
and years may pass before their meaning becomes clear — the
original happening being like the flash of light on film which,

to be made visible, must be developed by bathing in many solutions, and in the dark. Also, I was clanging inside with the misapprehensions of my education — my lack of it — about the "heathen" and his deities. My generation was taught virtually nothing about the Eastern world and the little that we did know was totally distorted by Western pride and condescension toward those "lesser breeds without the Law." What a joke! For a number of years I had been interested in Eastern religions and considered myself more than open-minded, yet now, with the tremendous impact of Elephanta, I heard again my missionary uncle's words of ridicule and horror: Why you know, they actually *worship idols!* Feasting on the grandeurs surrounding us, I was the child with a hand in the cookie jar, afraid of being caught — and I was also the adult, laughing. What was immediately clear, however, was that a particular "idol," or at least this one, can be a beacon and touchstone, visible evidence of things unseen as a tree is of the wind. Not till months later did I see that what had "come over me" and, apparently, over all of us in the dim cave was the inherence of spirit in matter, the presence of the unchanging and absolute in what is temporal and ephemeral. What else is that but "the kingdom of heaven within you"? In the Mahesamurti, God's presence, God immanent in Man, is made manifest. In a cave temple in India, the message of Christ is realized.

The German language has a beautiful word: *Innigkeit* — the sense of it somehow more inner than "innerness" — that comes close to what is in the faces at Elephanta, and the fact that the eyes are always closed or the eyelids lowered (except, interestingly, when Shiva is destroying) adds to the inherence. This indwellingness is double: the face is human and it is also divine; the face is in stone — boldly streaked in places with veins of different kinds of rock, striations of the earth itself — yet the stone is also spirit. Seeing substance and spirit so inseparably one, the familiar sense of being split into two dissolves away like the illusion it is.

For we live under a spell and don't know, or don't quite believe, that we do. It was laid on us as soon as we won the sense of our own identity and lost the sense of wholeness; it really took hold when we were taught about the paternal, external God who created heaven and earth (and us) and when we learned about all the things that take place in the "outside" world. Sometimes the spell is broken and we find ourselves, suddenly and dazzlingly, *in* the world, as if we had been asleep and were now awake. If only one could hold onto the moments of revelation, the lightning-bolt visions of reality! They are the "enlightenment" of the seer — the one who *sees* — they are the daylight in which he lives.

One thing remained — the shrine of the lingam which, to Hindus, is a true holy of holies. As Madhu had done in Nepal, so this guide too emphasized that Hinduism is a mono-theistic religion and that to the educated Hindu the different gods are only aspects of the one, undifferentiated Absolute. Now he went to great pains to explain that what appears to be worship of the phallus is, rather, worship of the creative principle of God — of the "universe of expanding forms." He spoke standing beside the shrine of the lingam — a cham-ber within the inner chamber, its floor plan a perfect mandala and the lingam itself silhouetted on three sides against light. With a mysterious smile, he then motioned to us to follow him and led us back to the central axis between the triple head and the opening of the cave.

"Look!" He pointed to the outside.

We turned and faced the entrance, eyes dazzled at first by the light. There, on the opposite shore, a structure dwarfing everything around it was the identical lingam shape: one of India's finest new nuclear reactors. The image of Shiva, partially destroyed in the temple, now faces, with eyes closed and with the compassion of divine inner peace, the potentially greatest destroyer of all. The two are in perfect opposition. Where is the creative imagination, the sense of irony fine enough to have brought that about?

*

We returned to Bombay and a farewell party with our traveling companions, who were about to scatter to Indonesia, East Africa, France. A little after midnight, the flight taking us to Rome roared into the sky, across the aisle from us the indefatigable Freddy with her misbehaving camera and amiable Bill, holding in his lap the hatbox tied with orange wool.

Between Hemispheres

BETWEEN HEMISPHERES

I RETURNED from the other side of the world, with a changed sense of time, as I tried rather futilely to explain, and a changed sense of self. You look different, a friend told me. Perhaps; one can't know — though it was odd that, after more than half a lifetime my hair chose to part itself on the opposite side of my head.

After a journey, first impressions of familiar places are as strange as what one left home to experience. Rome, for instance, which was the steppingstone on the way back, after where we'd been felt unbelievably young. Rome! That ancient empire was, to the East, as our own country is to Europe: an offshoot, a magnificently arrogant and enterprising youth bound on experimentation and assertion of newly discovered authority. How impressive its appearance was — so highly rational, planned, organized: the first Establishment!

Another leap, then, to the Western hemisphere, which seemed not so much the other side of the world as another planet altogether — or perhaps the same old planet at some faraway point in time. As we came in over eastern Long Island, the miles of suburban lots with their thousands of houses and the parking lots for millions of cars (their more

compressed, more rectangularly arranged versions), the loop-
ing traffic interchanges and shopping centers and high-rise
building complexes — all streaming past under the jet's wing
— weren't a "landscape" — had nothing to do with land.
What to call it, then: a manscape? No, for even from a
homing plane at a thousand feet, man was invisible and down
there at his level would be only a little less so: a totally
encased figure glimpsed in a pattern of traffic or known to
exist in the box or system of boxes in which he lives. A
structurescape, perhaps. Or, simply, a construction? It
seemed more. The crystal structure of Manhattan, when this
finally appeared in thickly hazed sunlight, was an awesome
aggregation, growing onto itself as if through the agency of
some organic compound, the two oversized crystals at its base
distorting and throwing off the balance of the whole — the
compound gone wild. Closer, coming in was like drifting
over a vast coral reef; rigid yet cellular, inhabited, the inhabitants invisible.

We arrived in the city, where they could be seen, and the
inhabitants looked as if they had no relation to the buildings
towering above them. They crowded, hurrying and purposeful, along the base of the buildings on walks made for them,
the flow jerkily detained by the imposed rhythms of traffic
lights; they entered and left enormous structures which dominated and appeared to control them as if these had been
designed and built not by people like themselves but by some
invisible superpower.

Night transfigured the buildings and made them still more
unreal: that sky-held glitter and glow was the extravagant
fancy of a dream being dreamt by millions, enthralling them
and so holding them asleep. Looking at their great presences

was to sense a dizzy-making paradox: these largest, most ingenious buildings the world has yet contrived are perhaps the most ephemeral. In a very few years it may be impossible to satisfy their monstrous appetites while the reason for their existence — that superpower that dreamed them up into the sky — may have moved into quite other concerns, or even dissolved. Increasingly the earth is forcing on its inhabitants recognition of and respect for its realities; like the occupants of the overblown palaces of Fatehpur Sikri, they begin to see their only water vanishing from the blistering plain, they sense uneasily that the "saint" that brought them there has died. Even more, the whole system that built and filled these monuments of "heroic materialism" shows signs of being as transitory as some of its products — those synthetics that vanish into air like a conjuror's trick when exposed to too much heat. Standing at the chilly black window that November night, among those beautiful illuminated monuments, I felt they were just that. In fact they already looked obsolete. Shafts and cliffs of steel and glass rooted in the island's rock, they were evanescent as bubbles. In the warm room I shivered. *"On sense l'automne qui vient."*

The suburbs offered a different kind of surprise and their own paradox. Driving in and out of the city, I was accustomed to passing areas of development houses that usually attracted no attention or else depressed me with their sameness. Now, I couldn't believe their pleasing appearance, their setting of well-kept grass and shrubbery and pavement, the garage or carport (the car off somewhere, no one around) with a hose coiled by a faucet (that ready water!), the draperies at every window and TV aerial on the roof. Why, these "average" homeowners were rich beyond belief! Were their lives as human beings reasonably enriched too? Their hearts and feelings nourished? I remembered the reaction of a Norwegian sea captain years ago when he sailed up the Connecticut River in his own ship for his first visit to a daughter newly married into a well-to-do Hartford family. Entertained in a succession of pleasant, biggish houses, he grew increasingly silent and thoughtful, finally asking a fellow Scandinavian, "Tell me — are these women *happy* with their big houses and all those possessions?" What would he have made of the miles of suburban homes filled with conveniences, their occupants the ideal consumer — "target" of advertisers competing with each other at "zeroing in" for the highest number of "hits"? It is no accident that the jargon used is identical to that of the military, intent on bombing the villages of Southeast Asia "back into the Stone Age." Here is the aggressive, masculine principle gone berserk — in love with its own potency, totally unrelated to persons whether in the gunsights of a bomber or in advertising charts of millions of people "sold."

As surroundings looked different on getting home, so also my inner landscape felt different. For quite some time I continued, surprisingly, to live in what I can best describe as a larger inner space, felt it almost physically — like another element in which I moved. During this period I noticed that I never felt in a hurry: I might clean up in the kitchen or pack a bag fast because I wanted to do it that way but the devil was not yet behind me. The whole subject of time sense is a tricky one and I tried to figure this out but the closest I could come to it was the feeling: Time is all here; I am in it and permeated by it as a fish is in water, as I am in the air. In this sense, consciousness felt quite literally expanded and in that different space, Time was nonlinear. Why was this so? What had happened?

We had been returned to the continuity of the human race in a part of the world where much of what has happened to humanity is still there to be experienced. In the wandering tribes of Iran and Afghanistan, the horsemen of central Asia, the water farming of Kashmir and the whole of Nepal, in the creaturely pace and ancient religious practices wherever they are found, the past is still intensely alive. In such settings, too, the monuments of the past are still rich with meaning where, with us, they are being steadily diminished by highways and high-rise, airplanes and automobiles until they bear almost no recognizable relationship to the present but become ever-shrinking islands in the twentieth century's violent sea. Without such distractions one is free to participate, however briefly and superficially, in that living past — see it evolve from nomadic to agricultural living, stare into the eyes of Alexander's conquests and Genghis Khan's forays. Man's deepest intuitions, myths and deities, carved into stone and still being presented with offerings, speak to one's own emptiness and searching. Returned to the unbroken continuity of history, one is made more whole oneself.

Several times in this account I have mentioned the surprise of touching what I suppose to be the Collective Unconscious and of suddenly resonating in some part of my being to the most outwardly alien people and customs. The caravan outside Kabul, the sacrifices at Dakshinkali and all the bizarre iconography of Nepal stirred regions of self I didn't know existed. On a more obvious level were experiences of connectedness (in spite of their strangeness) with Iranians in bazaars, villagers in India, rice harvesters in the Kathmandu valley. The linkage was double, or triple: with the ancient past, with foreign strangers, and with regions of myself. More and more I wondered and questioned what that "self" might possibly be and what it encompassed.

The term Collective Unconscious is somewhat misleading and at best an elusive concept, as Jungians are the first to agree. Jung himself was very careful not to say what it was, since nobody, of course, can know — however vivid and startling may be the images and archetypes that it produces. If I were to conjecture, as many have done before me, it suggests itself as being a limitless inner space or world of incredible richness, whose existence I am aware of only because of the images and ideas which come out of it; inner because it is invisible and I cannot locate it; inner also because it is I who intimately experience it, although it may not be inner at all but surrounding us and surrounding the earth — like those marvelously peopled auras and nimbuses of Tibetan mandalas and medieval heavens.

Before this trip I still assumed a somewhat limited attitude toward those parts of my mind, or being, of which I was not directly conscious: they were *my* past, *my* inheritance, the forgotten residue of my own mind — admittedly complex and accountable for sometimes violent and quite inexplicable feelings or behavior, but still very much mine. Because of Asia I began to sense how much more vast than can be imagined this world of invisible reality and unknown content must be, as much more so as "Outer Space" is greater than the visible sky on a day of high cloud cover, or better yet: as Outer Space is greater than the sky in one's immediate range of vision, from where one happens to be on the earth's surface.

Apparently the manifold glimpses Asia gives us of the

living past galvanize that invisible reality and may produce such intimations as that which first startled me at Persepolis, of the past still happening, of the connectedness through time of all humanity. And this wholly surrounding (or filling) world feels as though it might be nothing less than the continuing existence, the timeless presence, of humanity's entire experience. If this is so, then all of us on earth are, in truth, connected to one another; that invisible world is where we meet and what we share: it is both our common memory and the "Heavenly City of God" we are engaged in building whether we know it or not, simply by being alive, and here.

The thought is too awesome to grasp. Yet is there anyone who hasn't at some time been haunted by what happens to the live instant once it is past? Had that nagging wonder: where do the sounds of music go, or any experience that was intensely felt? what became of the children we once were, the loving we have done?

The miracle, and the mystery, of their being stored in individual memory exists; it seems possible, then, that nothing however great or small — nothing that happens anywhere — is lost, ever, but is instead transmuted, stored, abstracted in ways we cannot conceive of. In India there is a concept of such a record — the so-called *Akash* — in which everything that has happened in the universe has its etheric image in space — a kind of vast hall of light, a crystal. Poets, too, have tried to imagine it, as W. J. Turner did:

> *In Time like glass the stars are set,*
> *And seeming-fluttering butterflies*
> *Are fixed fast in Time's glass net*
> *With mountains and with maids' bright eyes.*
>
> .   .   .   .

The Himalayas' white, rapt brows;
The jewel-eyed bear that threads their caves;
The lush plains' lowing herds of cows;
That Shadow entering human graves:

All these like stars in Time are set,
They vanish but can never pass;
The Sun that with them fades is yet
Fast-fixed as they in Time like glass.

Increasingly it seems likely to me, and this was the gift of Asia, first announced in a dream, that just as nothing that has happened to any one of us is ever lost to him, so everything that has ever happened *is* — somewhere. But not in time as we know it or feel it in daily life; not in passing time but in that further dimension of time which we feel as timelessness: Time's heaven. To have this enter consciousness in anything but flashes and intimations would be as devastating as for the eye to gaze at the sun, but perhaps that other world, the counterpart of ordinary reality, plays on successive generations of humanity — becomes their thought and enters their dreaming, springing from the inexhaustible reservoirs of the collected, and collecting, Past.

Shortly after getting home I wrote to a friend that that other side of the world was also "the other side of consciousness, as if one walked into dreams." It isn't necessary to go as far as Kipling's "never the twain shall meet" to recognize that the East remained one way and the West developed into another, virtually mirror opposite. What was not yet possible in Kipling's day (or the possibility not recognized) is that the experience of Asia may cause these opposites, these two contrasting yet complementary heritages of man, to meet each other in the individual. His logical, enterprising and aggressive side may confront for the first time that "other side of consciousness" which is contemplative and intuitive, in touch with the earth and with unseen powers; more concerned with being than with doing. Reintroduced to another part of himself that is historically older and therefore less accessible, he sinks back into a continuity of consciousness lost, perhaps, when migrations began and races scattered to become themselves and live out their own separate destinies and histories. This is a part of the mind of which reasoning and industrious Western humanity is scarcely aware. Asia, wrote Jung, is the Unconscious of the West.

He believed, too, that in modern man consciousness has been overstressed to the point where an unbalanced situation has developed. The modern attitude (he wrote) "entirely forgets that it carries the whole living past in the lower stories of the skyscraper of rational consciousness. Without the lower stories it is as though our mind is suspended in mid-air. No wonder it gets nervous . . . The more powerful and independent consciousness becomes, and with it the conscious will, the more is the unconscious forced into the background until consciousness gets so far out of touch . . . as to make collapse inevitable."

The skyscraper of the Western mind has gone so high we may not be able to sustain it much longer. In a supreme triumph of conscious will and of the masculine principle it has gone to the moon and created a technology of fairy-tale powers; it has also invented and accumulated what it astonishingly calls a "safe" storehouse of self-destruct devices: at last publicized count fifteen times more than enough to kill us all.

Forced into the background by all this accomplishment and

the stupendous expenditure of energy it involves, is that other side of us that carries the whole living past in its depths and therefore connects us to one another — that "Unconscious of the West" which the traveler to Asia senses.

What good is that? We do not want to, and cannot, go back; we are Western, not Asian; we cannot all visit Asia. We don't need to: the East is in us — indissolubly part of us, a quality and a region of the mind.

This could be even more literally true than we imagine: discoveries made in neuropsychology and brain surgery indicate a remarkable counterpart to East and West in the two hemispheres of the brain. For over a century it has been known that the dominant hemisphere is associated with left- or right-handedness and is where the function of speech is located. Its way of thinking is logical, linguistic, propositional and, like the digital computer, its propositions work on the simple principle of opposites: zero or one, this or that. The importance of this discovery about the brain overshadowed the significance of the other, "inferior" hemisphere which, it appears, is strong in exactly the areas where the dominant one is weak — that is, in visualization, tonality and tonal memory, music — and analogy. This hemisphere's way of functioning is to combine, order, identify with — very much like the "analog computer," which we also invented.

Presumably these two ways of thinking, or of apprehending reality, have always existed in us though given varying importance in different ages and cultures. In a society like our present one in the West, rational thought is given supreme value, the other kind of thinking is considered strange, even suspect. It is quite obvious that we have become overspecialized in logical thought — in what we think of as masculine traits of mind — but the fact that the other kind is also actually in us even if now dormant and "inferior," is full of implications and suggestions for a synthesis, a transformation of consciousness. As Patrick Milburn, the reviewer of Joseph Bogen's recent papers about these "Two Different Minds" concluded, the unity we seek, which can embrace poetry and logic, the aesthetic and the conceptual, the East and the West, can perhaps be seen most fundamentally as a balance of the two sides of our own nature. Roland Fischer, an expert in brain function, adds: "The trip between the two hemispheres may be the longest in the Universe."

Maybe not — if we're ready to take it, or driven to it, if the skyscraper of the Western mind is about to topple. "I think we are seeing the *latter* stages of the rapid decline of Western civilization," our friend had said on a hillside in Switzerland.

But if much of what the West has created and valued is indeed dying, there are also signs of a growing spiritual awareness of the planet, a kind of planetary consciousness trying to be born — as Teilhard de Chardin envisaged twenty years ago in the remarkable *Phenomenon of Man*. Already his sweeping vision of a progressively convergent consciousness, wrapping and enfolding the globe until it eventually becomes a World-Mind, seems more real than when he presented it, the intensification of interdependence and communication far greater. Exactly what that World-Mind will be is as difficult to imagine, however, as it is to perceive the nature of any great historical change while living in the middle of it: you can't stand off and get a good look. (I remember as a young girl, on my first ocean voyage, longing to be able to look back from some point out over the waves at our ship moving through the water — the same longing, in miniature, now assuaged for all of earth's voyagers by photographs from space. It is interesting that the astronauts speak in reverent, almost mystical terms of nothing being the same after that look at the earth, as though, perhaps, they had achieved planetary consciousness.)

Everyday examples of increasing world-connectedness — a tightening of the web of collective consciousness — are so many and so common we scarcely notice them any more. At the same time the most horrifying random and impersonal violence and distrust appear to be increasing too, probably because we are terrified — in mortal terror of recognizing what we don't dare acknowledge: that we are in fact, innately, all brothers, as filled as ever with hostilities and aggressions, yet who *have* to get along: there's nowhere else to go.

As long as there were still oceans and mountain ranges to put between people's past and future, there was an "out," a horizon wide and far enough for the most immense hopes, fears or regrets. No wonder space exploration — the biggest "out" of all — came when it did and along with it a flurry of Jack-in-the-Beanstalk wish-thinking: maybe "out there," on the moon . . . on Mars . . . another world, another chance? A hen that lays golden eggs? Instead, there came reports of utter cold, utter lifelessness and, back toward home, the sight of that small blue ball — after which not just the astronauts but none of us will ever again be quite the same.

Meanwhile, here, we are seeing the related phenomenon of vastly more traveling about the earth itself, not entirely to be accounted for by affluence or the urge to see sights. Something else would seem to be afoot of which this is only the outward sign; as Laurens Van der Post put it: a long-arrested journey within the mind of man has begun again.

And an age-old journey is being intensified. Now, with the settling of the last "new" world by pioneers and refugees from the East and the loss of the last frontier, the circle around the earth is being drawn closer and closer. The West Coast of the United States, which always looked toward the Far East, has almost become western Asia; East and West have literally met, and at the historical moment when qualities that developed the West to what it is have become so over-grown and top-heavy they threaten to destroy their own creation.

What hardships, catastrophes, dark ages may be in store no one can predict though everyone can guess. The Dance of Shiva continues through vast spaces of history; the different aspects of Shiva come and go like light and dark. Early agri-cultural and village patterns, innerness of being and closeness to gods — all the expressions of the creative feminine energy of the Universe — grow into their own opposites, move out-ward in exploration and conquest, burst into the grandeur and triumph of reason and science. Are they about to re-turn, at another level, in a new form?

The more physics discovers about the nature of the uni-verse, the greater appears to be its immateriality: as if it were nothing else *but* a dance of energy at unimaginable seeds. "The stuff of the world is mind-stuff," as Eddington put it, and Sir James Jeans said that "the universe begins to look more like a great thought than a great machine." Meanwhile our inventions tend toward greater speeds and, for us, an abstracting of experience. We watch images of events, we communicate and transact at a distance, we move about in increasing insulation; substantive experience begins to approach that *Maya*, or play of illusions, believed in the East to be the nature of what we think of as reality. What does this mean? And what does it mean that time itself seems to be speeding up — as though the "Great Lord" danced more furiously? It would appear that the world seethes toward a boiling point, as though Life's essence, consciousness, were approaching some transformation: a different view of itself in the cosmos, a new way of apprehending.

And this, basically, it seems to me, is what the Counter-Culture, with all its ramifications, dead ends and unfortunate by-products has been about. From those flamboyant beginnings in California — Asia of the West — and its first bizarre manifestations elsewhere, it initiated and rapidly disseminated not only ways of living quite opposite to those of the Western world in general but a whole different way of seeing — induced at the beginning of the movement by hallucinogenic drugs with their sad train of evils but now by a variety of the strictest disciplines. The most unexpected and conventional communities are seeing a rise in meditation and yoga and other esoteric practices; the use of new (and also very old) techniques of getting into touch with the inner world, other than talking about it, is spreading. Throughout, there seems to be a growing recognition that there are realms of experience beyond the purely cognitive which we need to explore, not in order to be mindless but to be more whole.

At crucial times in history before this, people have turned to the occult. The interesting thing now is that science itself is making such matters as astrology, sorcery and supersensory phenomena more legitimate. Superstition used to attribute the disposition of beings and events to "the stars" but the more is

known about the universe and the Unified Field, the more
difficult it becomes to pooh-pooh these mysteries. "The
Universe is not only queerer than we suppose but queerer
than we can suppose," as Haldane said.

Certainly very strange things indeed are happening when
we go to the moon and discover the earth; invent computers
and learn about the brain; wake up to find an instrument of
entertainment becoming a form of public conscience. It is as
though in spite of our doings — almost in proportion to how
extreme these are — we are being continually edged in another direction, by forces of which we know virtually nothing. Toward what? A closer and more intimate connection
to essence rather than substance? A different reality from
that which we think of as reality?

I admit to being as perplexed as the next person by what I
see, swinging alternately between dread, sometimes convic-
tion, of impending doom — and dreams, sometimes certainty, of unimaginable renaissance — a quite plausible position, it seems to me, in an extreme situation of excess such
as we are in. For extremity is the only certainty: we cannot
continue in the way we are going. Much more of the same
anything — growth, technology, and (particularly) passion
for power and for independence — and we're undone. The
only true hope is in the most radical change of all: a change in
consciousness.

Mariners used to sense unseen landfalls from a variety of
clues: subtle changes of temperature and sea, a new smell in
the air, an escort of shore birds. In navigating dangerous
waters perhaps, like them, we should pay careful heed to
those elements which differ from the expected and usual in
our perceptions and interpretations: to the random and unex-

plained, the coincidences which seem more than chance, the way things happen without our doing and in clusters of meaning (the person one meets at exactly the right moment; any succession of extremely pertinent "small" events). What is this operative chance? Which, like Heisenberg's "imp" in physics, goes counter to the expected, the rule, the "science proves . . ." attitude to which we are enslaved? Even more, what occurs when we let go, relax excessive willfulness, watch and listen?

We continue to subdivide time into smaller and smaller units of sharply focused attention: those moments in the phone booth, scrambling for change; the split-second appraisals of clearance between sixty-mile-an-hour cars; just as open space is being cut into smaller and smaller lots. We might do well to notice, and invite, any states of being that achieve the opposite effect, that combine and make whole, enlarge our awareness, that take us out of time and transform the familiar. I think of the afternoon on a balcony in Kabul, just looking; the listening from a gimcrackery houseboat in Kashmir to the everyday sounds of people living; the extraordinarily simple joy of meditating with a group of strangers on a hilltop in Nepal — and a host of similar experiences right at home, in less exotic surroundings but just as marvelous in their effect of making ordinary life magic. At such times, "nothing special" as the Zen Buddhist puts it, turns out to be simply everything. And always is? We are overtaken by the wild surmise: perhaps we are already, each one of us, World Mind.